Contemporary Scenes for Actors
Men

Michael Earley was Chief Producer of Plays for BBC Radio Drama in London. He was Chairman of the Theatre Studies Program at Yale University and taught acting, dramatic literature and playwriting there and at New York University's Tisch School of the Arts, the Juilliard School's Acting Program, Smith College and various other schools and universities in America and Britain. He is publisher of Methuen Drama.

Philippa Keil has edited seven books for Methuen including *Contemporary Scenes for Actors* (Women), *The Contemporary Monologue* (Women and Men), *The Modern Monologue* (Women and Men) and *The Classical Monologue* (Women and Men). She is also a freelance writer, editor and translator who trained at the Yale School of Drama. She graduated from Sussex University where she acted, directed and produced plays for the Frontdoor Theatre, and then worked professionally in London at Richmond's Orange Tree Theatre and in America with her own company Ballet Cirque.

by the same authors

Contemporary Scenes for Actors (Women)
The Contemporary Monologue (Women and Men)
The Modern Monologue (Women and Men)
The Classical Monologue (Women and Men)
Soliloquy! The Shakespeare Monologues (Women and Men)
Solo: The Best Monologues of the 80s (Women and Men)

Contemporary Scenes for Actors
Actors
Men

Edited with notes and commentaries by

MICHAEL EARLEY
& PHILIPPA KEIL

Routledge/Theatre Arts Books
New York

1 3 5 7 9 10 8 6 4 2

First published in the United Kingdom in 1999 by
Methuen Publishing Limited

Published in the USA and Canada by
Routledge/Theatre Arts Books
29 West 35th Street
New York, NY 10001
www.routledge–ny.com

A CIP catalogue record for this book is available from the Library of
Congress

ISBN 0 878 30077 5

Typeset by Deltatype Ltd, Birkenhead, Merseyside

Printed and bound in Great Britain by
Cox & Wyman Ltd, Reading, Berks

Contents

Notes to the Actors

This book of scenes, arranged specifically for actors who are working together, offers a selection of pieces from some of the most energetic and exciting plays of the past few years. As we enter the new millennium, the contemporary theatre has suddenly revitalised itself and is attracting a whole new generation of young dramatists who are capturing the imagination of performers and audiences on both sides of the Atlantic. These writers are producing muscular, compelling and often controversial plays which are finding favour in both the commercial and subsidised theatres. These dramas, often set against a backdrop of urban ennui and violence, share common chords of disaffection, anger and angst. The dramatic tones of these works vary from the bleaky tragic to the openly farcical, offering a rich range of parts into which actors can really sink their teeth.

The scenes in this volume provide a representative cross-section from a whole range of recent British, American and Irish plays. We have applied strict criteria in our selection process so that we could give actors all-round scenes, which will work in the classroom, audition room or rehearsal studio. Professional actors have proved in performance every one of the plays from which we have chosen material. Some have had further productions since their premieres. They also work as pieces of writing independent of a particular performance and performers. Since all of the plays from which the scenes are derived are in print, we cannot stress too strongly the importance of reading and being familiar with the whole play before you begin work. In fact, you must work through the play as often as possible to gain the full context of both the characters and their dramatic situation. Scenes provide links between a play's key stages. The actor must know where the character is coming from and where the character is heading towards before making complete sense of a character's journey through the play. Something in the first or last part of a script may hold a vital clue for understanding the scene on which you are working. So connect your scene to others as you work.

We have also selected scenes which we think work because each, in their own way, is a mini-drama with its own beginning, middle and end. This is a crucial feature of any good scene. In performing the material it helps when you can actually follow a single arc of action or sequence of events which appear to have an independent life from the rest of the play. All the information and details given to the actors about the characters create a story which then integrates with the other stories told in the play. We judge a play by the way its various plot strands either confirm or contradict the knowledge we receive scene by scene. The tension that results from this rich interplay of narrative results in drama.

We have tried to ensure that each of the characters has an equal stake in the scene. In some instances a character's silent presence and unspoken reactions offer an acting challenge equal to that of a verbal character. Not every character needs to speak volumes in order to hold the stage.

In thinking about his or her character, the actor can come to the task with a whole range of questions that can allow you to uncover a wealth of details embedded in the text. The following are but a few simple suggestions to help you begin this uncovering process for yourself:

- *Who am I?* The big question which this scene might only partly answer. The rest of the play, however, will shed further light. Be careful, however, of information which might lead to self-delusion or give you a false sense of self.
- *What do I want?* In every scene the character is trying to achieve something, to get something from another character on-stage. As characters play against each other they can throw up obstacles which need to be deflected. How to deal with these obstacles is part of the acting challenge.
- *What is my status?* This can often be a key question when trying to get inside a character. Characters are often matched or mismatched according to their status in life: masters and

servants, parents and children, men and women, etc. The chemistry between characters often starts with this basic question.

- *How articulate am I?* This is a useful question to ask especially where text is concerned. We are what we speak, and you can often pursue a rich exploration of character by looking at the kind of language they use. Some characters have a fluid ease with words but may use them as a mask. Other characters may be verging on the inarticulate, but use the few words they possess with unusual power and passion.

- *How well do we work together?* This is a crucial question for both actors working on a scene together. It can often lead directly to uncovering the dynamics which propel a scene. Are you friends or enemies? Do you love or hate each other? Are you trying to help or deny one another? You can ask an endless series of simple and more complicated questions like these in order to delve deeper and deeper into the on-stage relationship.

As actors you should prepare your own agenda of further questions in order to explore not only your own character but also the nature of your on-stage relationship with your partner.

So much about scene work is wrestling with the qualities offered by a two-character scene. Unlike a monologue, where you are acting alone on-stage and project outwards to an audience, in a scene the acting energy is far less presentational and more concentrated on a relationship. You have to learn to act together, not separately. Actors in a scene make a pact to work in concert, even when the scene seems to be pulling time apart. You search the script together for collaborative cues which allow each of you to pick up from one another and pass the baton back and forth. A scene can often be like a relay race. You will begin to notice that timing and rhythm – how you play together back and forth – begin to enter into the process. The more knowledge each of you shares about the scene the better the job you'll perform together.

We have designed this volume to work in tandem with *Contemporary Scenes for Actors: Women*. The introductions for each scene provide the basic set-up and character information to launch you into the specific action. Each scene is then followed by a commentary, which is not intended as acting or director's notes but is meant to highlight some useful features and details in the scene. But the actors must do the real work of asking the important questions and uncovering any scene's dynamic for themselves. Clearly this will change with each new pairing of actors. We want to stress again that there can be no substitute for reading the entire play. Without doing so you risk only getting a piece of the action, a part of the story, a selected view of the characters. Any scene can only be a part of the whole. The Play Sources will direct you to the full version of each text.

Michael Earley
Philippa Keil
London 1999

Scenes for One Man and One Woman

The Beauty Queen of Leenane
Martin McDonagh

Act I, scene 3. The living-room kitchen of a rural cottage in the west of Ireland. Night. Set only just illuminated by the orange coals through the bars of the range. Radio has been left on low in the kitchen.

Maureen Folan is 'a plain, slim woman of about forty' and Pato Dooley is 'a good-looking man, aged about forty'. He has been working as a casual labourer on building sites in England and has come back to Ireland for a brief visit to 'say hello and goodbye' to his 'Yankee' relatives. Maureen lives at home with Mag, her aged hypochondriac mother, tending their isolated small holding. These two women co-exist in a constant state of hate, resentment and bitterness. The harsh loneliness of their poor rural surroundings has an inexorable influence over their lives. At the age of twenty-five, while working as a cleaner, Maureen had a nervous breakdown. Mag's response to this, as she never fails to remind Maureen, was to have her put away in a 'nut-house' for a month. In this scene, Maureen is bringing Pato home late in the evening after a party for his American relatives. This is the first time we see these two characters together. They have known one another since they were children but have never been romantically involved. As the scene starts 'footsteps and voices of Maureen and Pato are heard outside, both slightly drunk'.

PATO (*off, singing*). 'The Cadillac stood by the house . . .'
MAUREEN (*off*). Shh, Pato . . .
PATO (*off. Singing quietly*). 'And the Yanks they were within.' (*Speaking.*) What was it that oul fella used to say, now?
MAUREEN (*off*). What oul fella, now?

3

(MAUREEN *opens the door and the two of them enter, turning the lights on.* MAUREEN *is in a new black dress, cut quite short.* PATO *is a good-looking man of about the same age as her.*)

PATO. The oul fella who used to chase oul whatyoucall. Oul Bugs Bunny.

MAUREEN. Would you like a cup of tea, Pato?

PATO. I would.

(MAUREEN *switches the kettle on.*)

MAUREEN. Except keep your voice down, now.

PATO (*quietly*). I will, I will. (*Pause.*) I can't remember *what* he used to say. The oul fella used to chase Bugs Bunny. It was something, now.

MAUREEN. Look at this. The radio left on too, the daft oul bitch.

PATO. Sure, what harm? No, leave it on, now. It'll cover up the sounds.

MAUREEN. What sounds?

PATO. The smooching sounds.

(*He gently pulls her to him and they kiss a long while, then stop and look at each other. The kettle has boiled.* MAUREEN *gently breaks away, smiling, and starts making the tea.*)

MAUREEN. Will you have a biscuit with your tea?

PATO. I will. What biscuits do you have, now?

MAUREEN. Em, only Kimberleys.

PATO. I'll leave it so, Maureen. I do hate Kimberleys. In fact I think Kimberleys are the most horrible biscuits in the world.

MAUREEN. The same as that, I hate Kimberleys. I only get them to torment me mother.

PATO. I can't see why the Kimberley people go making them at all. Coleman Connor ate a whole pack of Kimberleys one time and he was sick for a week. (*Pause.*) Or was it Mikados? It was some kind of horrible biscuits.

4

MAUREEN. Is it true Coleman cut the ears off Valene's dog and keeps them in his room in a bag?

PATO. He showed me them ears one day.

MAUREEN. That's awful spiteful, cutting the ears off a dog.

PATO. It *is* awful spiteful.

MAUREEN. It would be spiteful enough to cut the ears off anybody's dog, let alone your own brother's dog.

PATO. And it had seemed a nice dog.

MAUREEN. Aye. (*Pause.*) Aye.

(*Awkward pause. PATO cuddles up behind her.*)

PATO. You feel nice to be giving a squeeze to.

MAUREEN. Do I?

PATO. Very nice.

(MAUREEN *continues making the tea as* PATO *holds her. A little embarrassed and awkward, he breaks away from her after a second and idles a few feet away.*)

MAUREEN. Be sitting down for yourself, now, Pato.

PATO. I will. (*Sits at table.*) I do do what I'm told, I do.

MAUREEN. Oh-ho, do you now? That's the first time tonight I did notice. Them stray oul hands of yours.

PATO. Sure, I have no control over me hands. They have a mind of their own. (*Pause.*) Except I didn't notice you complaining overmuch anyways, me stray oul hands. Not too many complaints at all!

MAUREEN. I had complaints when they were straying over that Yank girl earlier on in the evening.

PATO. Well, I hadn't noticed you there at that time, Maureen. How was I to know the beauty queen of Leenane was still yet to arrive?

MAUREEN. 'The beauty queen of Leenane.' Get away with ya!

PATO. Is true!

MAUREEN. Why so have no more than two words passed between us the past twenty year?

5

Sure, it's took me all this time to get up the

REEN (*smiling*). Ah, bollocks to ya!

O *smiles*. MAUREEN *brings the tea over and sits down*.)

PATO. I don't know, Maureen. I don't know.

MAUREEN. Don't know what?

PATO. Why I never got around to really speaking to you or asking you out or the like. I don't know. Of course, hopping across to that bastarding oul place every couple of months couldn't've helped.

MAUREEN. England? Aye. Do you not like it there so?

PATO (*pause*). It's money. (*Pause.*) And it's Tuesday I'll be back there again.

MAUREEN. Tuesday? This Tuesday?

PATO. Aye. (*Pause.*) It was only to see the Yanks off I was over. To say hello and say goodbye. No time back at all.

MAUREEN. That's Ireland, anyways. There's always someone leaving.

PATO. It's always the way.

MAUREEN. Bad, too.

PATO. What can you do?

MAUREEN. Stay?

PATO (*pause*). I do ask meself, if there was good work in Leenane, would I stay in Leenane? I mean, there never will be good work, but hypothetically, I'm saying. Or even bad work. Any work. And when I'm over there in London and working in rain and it's more or less cattle I am, and the young fellas cursing over cards and drunk and sick, and the oul digs over there, all pee-stained mattresses and nothing to do but watch the clock . . . when it's there I am, it's here I wish I was, of course. Who wouldn't? But when it's here I am . . . it isn't *there* I want to be, of course not. But I know it isn't here I want to be either.

6

MAUREEN. And why, Pato?

PATO. I can't put my finger on why. (*Pause.*) Of course it's beautiful here, a fool can see. The mountains and the green, and people speak. But when everybody knows everybody else's business . . . I don't know. (*Pause.*) You can't kick a cow in Leenane without some bastard holding a grudge twenty year.

MAUREEN. It's true enough.

PATO. It is. In England they don't care if you live or die, and it's funny but that isn't altogether a bad thing. Ah, sometimes it is . . . ah, I don't know.

MAUREEN (*pause*). Do you think you'll ever settle down in the one place so, Pato? When you get married, I suppose.

PATO (*half-laughing*). 'When I get married . . .'

MAUREEN. You will someday, I'll bet you, get married. Wouldn't you want to?

PATO. I can't say it's something I do worry me head over.

MAUREEN. Of course, the rake of women you have stashed all over, you wouldn't need to.

PATO (*smiling*). I have no rake of women.

MAUREEN. You have one or two, I bet.

PATO. I may have one or two. That I know to say hello to, now.

MAUREEN. Hello me . . . A-hole.

PATO. Is true. (*Pause.*) Sure, I'm no . . .

MAUREEN (*pause*). No what?

(*Pause. PATO shrugs and shakes his head, somewhat sadly. Pause. The song 'The Spinning Wheel', sung by Delia Murphy, has just started on the radio.*)

MAUREEN (*continued*). Me mother does love this oul song. Oul Delia Murphy.

PATO. This is a creepy oul song.

MAUREEN. It *is* a creepy oul song.

7

PATO. She does have a creepy oul voice. Always scared me this song did when I was a lad. She's like a ghoul singing. (*Pause.*) Does the grandmother die at the end, now, or is she just sleeping?

MAUREEN. Just sleeping, I think she is.

PATO. Aye . . .

MAUREEN (*pause*). While the two go hand in hand through the fields.

PATO. Aye.

MAUREEN. Be moonlight.

PATO (*nods*). They don't write songs like that any more. Thank Christ. (MAUREEN *laughs. Brighter.*) Wasn't it a grand night though, Maureen, now?

MAUREEN. It was.

PATO. Didn't we send them on their way well?

MAUREEN. We did, we did.

PATO. Not a dry eye.

MAUREEN. Indeed.

PATO. Eh?

MAUREEN. Indeed.

PATO. Aye. That we did. That we did.

MAUREEN (*pause*). So who *was* the Yankee girl you did have your hands all over?

PATO (*laughing*). Oh will you stop it with your 'hands all over'?! Barely touched her, I did.

MAUREEN. Oh-ho!

PATO. A second cousin of me uncle, I think she is. Dolores somebody. Healey or Hooley. Healey. Boston, too, she lives.

MAUREEN. That was illegal so if it's your second cousin she is.

PATO. Illegal me arse, and it's not *my* second cousin she is anyway, and what's so illegal? Your second cousin's boobs aren't out of bounds, are they?

MAUREEN. They are!

PATO. I don't know about that. I'll have to consult with me lawyer on that one. I may get arrested the next time. And I have a defence anyways. She had dropped some Taytos on her blouse, there, I was just brushing them off for her.

MAUREEN. Taytos me arsehole, Pato Dooley!

PATO. Is true! (*Lustful pause. Nervously.*) Like this is all it was . . .

(PATO *slowly reaches out and gently brushes at, then gradually fondles,* MAUREEN's *breasts. She caresses his hand as he's doing so, then slowly gets up and sits across his lap, fondling his head as he continues touching her.*)

MAUREEN. She was prettier than me.

PATO. You're pretty.

MAUREEN. She was prettier.

PATO. I like you.

MAUREEN. You have blue eyes.

PATO. I do.

MAUREEN. Stay with me tonight.

PATO. I don't know, now, Maureen.

MAUREEN. Stay. Just tonight.

PATO (*pause*). Is your mother asleep?

MAUREEN. I don't care if she is or she isn't. (*Pause.*) Go lower.

(PATO *begins easing his hands down her front.*)

Go lower . . . Lower . . .

(*His hands reach her crotch. She tilts her head back slightly. The song on the radio ends. Blackout.*)

COMMENTARY: Notice how unromantic the setting is; the offer of tea and 'Kimberleys' is not exactly the food of love. Mag is asleep upstairs, although she could well be awake and eavesdropping. The radio is randomly playing in the background to cover up the 'smooching sounds'. Both Maureen and Pato have come back with the same idea in mind, although they obviously have not talked about it. She wants him and he wants her but there is a preliminary wariness to be articulated first. Maureen appears to have the upper hand; to be controlling the situation, gently insinuating that Pato has taken his time in making his moves on her. She jealously reminds Pato of his earlier attentions towards the Yankee girl, but her harping on this subject could almost lose her Pato altogether. Maureen puts Pato in a position where he feels compelled to explain himself. Considering her relatively protected life and her lack of boyfriends – 'What have I ever done but *kissed* two men the past forty year' – she is remarkably confident with Pato. This is almost the reverse of the situation we would expect. Pato is certainly lustful, but is hampered by his tongue-tied shyness when challenged by Maureen's confident taunting wit. He is tenative and she knows just what she wants. He will deflect this with his talk about biscuits and assorted chit-chat. To help your performances you must decide just how experienced and confident these characters are in love and sex.

Boys' Life
Howard Korder

Act 1, scene 2. A large city. The present. A child's bedroom. Phil and Karen standing at opposite ends of the room, facing each other. The bed is piled with coats. Sounds of a party filter in from outside.

Phil (late 20s) works at a 9-to-5 job. He's neurotic and a hypochondriac. Phil has a dismal track record in his relationships with women, and his friends are used to hearing his 'sexual sob stories'. Finding a girlfriend has become an obsession for Phil. Karen (late 20s) is also neurotic and has a very low sense of self-esteem. Later in the play it is revealed that 'She says she's frigid . . . She says her uncle raped her when she was ten.' Unlike Phil, Karen is afraid of relationships and commitment. Several months ago this unlikely couple had a brief, two-night fling. In this scene they meet again for the first time.

PHIL. Well, there *you* are.
KAREN. Yes.
PHIL. And here I am.
KAREN. Yes.
PHIL. So here we are, both of us. Together.
KAREN. Talking.
PHIL. Right here in the same room.
KAREN. It's pretty amazing. (*Pause.*) Enjoying the party?
PHIL. Oh yes. Certainly. Yes yes yes.
KAREN. Mmmm.
PHIL. No.
KAREN. Oh.
PHIL. Not in the larger sense.

KAREN. Why did you come?

PHIL. I was invited. I mean . . . Jack invited me.

KAREN. And you do everything Jack says.

PHIL. No, I . . . he's my friend. My oldest friend. (*Pause.*) You look great tonight, Karen.

KAREN. Thanks.

PHIL. No, I mean it. Just wonderful. (*Pause.*)

KAREN. You look good.

PHIL. No.

KAREN. You do.

PHIL. No I don't.

KAREN. Really, you do.

PHIL. Do I?

KAREN. What do you want, Phil?

PHIL. Well, I don't *want* anything. I just wanted to . . . say hello.

KAREN. Hello.

PHIL. Yes, well. (*Pause.*) That's lovely, what you have on, what is it?

KAREN. A dress.

PHIL. I've always admired your sense of humor, Karen.

KAREN. What do you want, Phil? [(*The door opens and a* MAN *pops his head in.*)

MAN. Oh. I'm sorry.

KAREN. We're almost done.

MAN. Oh. Well. Fine. I'll, ah . . . fine. (*He exits, closing the door.*)

PHIL. What was that all about?

KAREN. What?

PHIL. That. That guy.

KAREN. I don't know.

PHIL. Well, you seemed pretty familiar with him.]

KAREN. Are you feeling okay?

PHIL. Hmm? Oh, sure. Things are going really really great for me right now. Just fine. I have my own partition

12

now, over at the office, they put up one of those, ah . . . so *that's* really good. And I'm going to the spa a lot, I'm working ou – well, I can't use the machines cause you know of my back, but I love the Jacuzzi, so, actually, it's strange, cause I fell asleep in it, in the whirlpool, and when I woke up I had this incredible headache, I mean it would *not* go away, I felt this thing here like the size of a peach pit, I went for a *blood* test, I was convinced I, you hear all this stuff now, the way it's spreading, I mean I'm not – but I was sure I had it.

KAREN. Had what?

PHIL. You know. (*Pause.*)

KAREN. And?

PHIL. I didn't. So. (*Pause.* KAREN *looks at the door.*) Anyway, it's funny we both happened to turn up here tonight, isn't it, cause I was just thinking. I was wondering . . . I mean, it's a couple of months since I last spoke to you and I was just *wondering* if we were still, you know, seeing each other.

KAREN. *Seeing* each other.

PHIL. Yes.

KAREN. No. (*Pause.*)

PHIL. All right.

KAREN. We were never seeing each other, Phil.

PHIL. Well, no, not actually *seeing* . . .

KAREN. We slept together once.

PHIL. Twice.

KAREN. You left before I woke up.

PHIL. Okay, yeah, but . . . I mean, *everybody* does that.

KAREN. And you never called.

PHIL. Now . . . now about *that*, you see, I was involved in a very bad kind of situation then, and I wasn't really in a position to, ah . . . as much as I *wanted* to . . . and I *did*, very, very –

KAREN. What do you want?

PHIL (*pause*). Well, I'd like another shot at it.

KAREN. At what?

PHIL. At you. To get to know you.

KAREN. I'm really not worth the effort, Phil.

PHIL. You're seeing someone else, right?

KAREN. That's got nothing to –

PHIL. You *are* seeing someone.

KAREN. Not actually *seeing* . . .

PHIL. No, no, it's fine. Early bird and all that stuff. I'm fine. Everything is fine.

KAREN. It's got nothing to do with you, Phil. There's just a lot of things I have to work through right now. But I like you, I do. You're . . . you're a wonderful person.

PHIL. You're a wonderful person too, Karen.

KAREN. Well, so are you, Phil.

PHIL. That's right. We both are. (*He hugs* KAREN.) Listen to this. A guy in my office has a cabin upstate. He never uses it. It's on the edge of a beautiful freshwater lake. Why don't we go there, just the two of us, we spend the weekend, relax, get out of the city . . . do some straight thinking. What do you say?

KAREN. No.

PHIL. Is it because of this guy you're seeing?

KAREN. Well, I'm not actually *seeing* –

PHIL. Then what is it?

KAREN. It's just not a good idea.

PHIL. It's not?

KAREN. No. Not at all. (*Pause.*) You're touching my breasts, Phil. [(*The* MAN *pops his head through the door.*)

MAN. Oh gosh. Beg pardon. (*He shuts the door.*)]

PHIL. I think about you a lot, Karen.

KAREN. You do.

PHIL. Yes. At work, you know, the laundromat, in the

shower . . . places like that. (*Pause.*) I mean that in the positive sense.

KAREN. I'm not worth the trouble.

PHIL. It's just two days out of your life, Karen. This could turn out to be something really special, it'll be over before you know it.

KAREN. You're making this very difficult.

PHIL. I'm making it incredibly *easy*. Come up to the country with me.

KAREN. Phil –

PHIL. Come.

KAREN. Please, Phil –

PHIL. I'm asking for a *chance*.

KAREN. Oh, no. Oh no. This is coming at a very bad time for me. I don't think I can handle this right now. My life is a real big mess, okay, and . . . I read that by the time you're five you've already developed the major patterns for the rest of your life. I mean whether you're going to be basically happy or . . . a fireman, a lesbian, whatever. And of course it's not fair at all, because nobody tells a little kid anything about that. But that's the way it is. So I've been thinking about this. And it occurs to me that somewhere along the line I screwed up really bad. I made a very poor choice about something and now there's nothing I can do to change it.

PHIL. I think I love you.

KAREN. You haven't even been listening.

PHIL. Of course I have. You were talking about your childhood, right? I love you.

KAREN. No, Phil. I'm really very flattered –

PHIL. I'm not saying it to flatter you, Karen. We're not talking about your drapes. We're talking about this very real and undeniable feeling I have for you. So you're not happy. I think I can sense that from what you just told me.

15

But *nobody's* happy. That's the way things are *supposed* to be. You think I'm happy? I'm not happy, I'm miserable.

KAREN. I am too.

PHIL. I know you are. That's why I feel so close to you. Karen? I can *make* you happy. And you can make me happy. We can help each other.

KAREN. You just said that nobody is happy.

PHIL. I didn't *mean* that. I feel so crazy when I'm with you I don't know what I'm saying. I love you.

KAREN. No – please –

PHIL. I love you. I'm sick with needing you. It's an actual disease. I'm all swollen and rotten inside, my brain is decomposing, and it's because of you.

KAREN. What's wrong with you, Phil?

PHIL. I'm dying without you, Karen. I'm serious. Has anyone ever told you anything like that? Ever?

KAREN. No. Never.

PHIL. Because no one has ever loved you as much as I do. Jesus, Karen, help me! [(*The* MAN *pops his head through the door.*)

MAN. Excuse me . . .

PHIL. What? What do you want?

MAN. Well . . . my coat . . .

PHIL. In a minute.

MAN. I've been waiting –

PHIL. GO AWAY! (*The* MAN *shuts the door.*)]
I love you.

KAREN. For how long?

PHIL. Until I'm in my grave. Longer. Forever.

KAREN. No, I mean . . . how long would we have to be away for?

PHIL. As long as you want. We don't even have to come back.

KAREN. I was thinking just the weekend.

PHIL. Yes, yes, the weekend. A day. An hour. A single second.

KAREN. I have pasta class Monday nights.

PHIL. Great. Fabulous. (*Pause.*)

KAREN. I wish I could, Phil. It's not that I don't want to . . .

PHIL. If you want to, just say yes. Don't worry about the rest.

KAREN. I can't.

PHIL. Then just say maybe.

KAREN. If I say maybe, you'll think I'm saying yes.

PHIL. I won't. I promise. I'm very clear on maybe. (*Pause.*) Please, Karen. Give me a crumb. Throw me a line.

KAREN. Oh, let me think about it. I have to . . . okay. Maybe. I'd like to – I don't know, maybe.

PHIL. Maybe. Maybe. Thank you, Karen. You won't be sorry. I'm crazy about you. You know that, don't you?

KAREN. I'm not worth it, Phil. Really.

PHIL. This is the happiest day of my life. (*He kisses her and eases her down onto the bed. He climbs on top of her and starts to caress her.* [*The* MAN *enters.*)

MAN. Look, I'm very sorry about this, but I need my coat.]

(KAREN *breaks away and sits on the edge of the bed.*)
[Sorry.

KAREN. That's all right. We're done.

MAN. Are you?]

PHIL (*rising from the bed*). Come on. Let's get back to the party.

KAREN. No, you go ahead.

PHIL. You're not coming?

KAREN. In a minute.

PHIL (*moving toward her*). Is everything okay?

17

KAREN. Yes, yes, it's really – Phil, no please, please, just stay away – [(*To the* MAN.) Look, I'm sorry, I – (*Turning away.*)]
Oh God I hate myself so *much!* (*She runs out of the room.*)
PHIL (*following her*). Karen, wait a – (*She slams the door.*) Shit. Shit shit shit! (*He leans against the door. Silence.*)

COMMENTARY: The playwright gives the actors very few concrete facts about either character. It may help you to try and create your own histories for them. Although this is the only scene in which Karen actually appears, Phil's infatuation and obsession with her only increase, at first in this scene and then as the play progresses. Notice the extremely unromantic setting in which the two find themselves – a child's bedroom that is being used as a dumping place for coats. It is important not to let the scene become too serious. The passion and tragedy all have an oddball edge as their self-absorption becomes ever more absurd. Phil is a natural gabbler with a tendency to run at the mouth. Every time Phil tries to break the ice Karen responds with a quirky question or sardonic observation. Despite her obvious reluctance and reticence he blunders on with increasing desperation. The scene opens with them isolated on either side of the stage but fairly quickly Phil not only engineers a hug, but also starts fondling Karen's breasts. It is important for the actors to choreograph the pace of this comic seduction. They both over-analyse and interpret each other's words and actions. She is underwhelmed by his overwhelming propositions and flattery. Notice that with each brush off from Karen, Phil becomes ever more desperate and verbose.

Broken Glass
Arthur Miller

Act I, scene 2. The Gellburg bedroom in a house in Brooklyn, New York. The last days of November 1938.

The Gellburgs, Sylvia (mid 40s) and Phillip (late 40s), have been married for over twenty years. For the past nine days she has been confined to a wheelchair suffering from a mysterious paralysis of her legs. She is a 'buxom, capable and warm woman. Right now her hair is brushed down to her shoulders, and she is in a nightgown and robe.' Soon after they were married their son Jerome was born. Following her son's birth Sylvia was eager to return to her job as a bookkeeper, but Phillip categorically refused to let her. By coincidence, at about the same time, Phillip suddenly became impotent. Over the years these two particular incidents have fuelled Sylvia's growing sense of resentment. She has maintained a passionate devotion to books, and has become increasingly obsessed with reading the papers for news of what is happening to the Jews in Nazi Germany. Phillip is a slender, intense man. 'He is in a black suit, black tie and shoes and white shirt.' Phillip works at the Brooklyn Guarantee and Trust, running their Mortgage Department. He is a workaholic, putting in ten or eleven hours a day at the office. Phillip is described as being an 'uptight little pisser'. He is proud of what he has achieved as a Jew in a predominantly gentile world, and yet 'he'd rather not be one'. This is not the happiest of marriages, and the absence of sex for the last twenty years due to Phillip's impotence has only aggravated things. Phillip is imbued with pent-up anger and a violent rage is kept just below the surface. As this scene starts Phillip returns home unexpectedly, following a secret consultation with Sylvia's doctor who has suggested that her illness may be due to a psychosomatic rather than a physical cause. Sylvia is reading a newspaper. 'Suddenly she turns in shock – Gellburg is standing behind her. He holds a small paper bag.'

SYLVIA. Oh! I didn't hear you come in.

GELLBURG. I tiptoed, in case you were dozing off . . . (*His dour smile.*) I bought you some sour pickles.

SYLVIA. Oh, that's nice! Later maybe. You have one.

GELLBURG. I'll wait. (*Awkwardly but determined.*) I was passing Greenberg's on Flatbush Avenue and I suddenly remembered how you used to love them. Remember?

SYLVIA. Thanks, that's nice of you. What were you doing on Flatbush Avenue?

GELLBURG. There's a property across from A&S. I'm probably going to foreclose.

SYLVIA. Oh that's sad. Are they nice people?

GELLBURG (*shrugs*). People are people – I gave them two extensions but they'll never manage . . . nothing up here. (*Taps his temple.*)

SYLVIA. Aren't you early?

GELLBURG. I got worried about you. Doctor come?

SYLVIA. He called; he has results of the tests but he wants to come tomorrow when he has more time to talk to me. He's really very nice.

GELLBURG. How was it today?

SYLVIA. I'm so sorry about this.

GELLBURG. You'll get better, don't worry about it. Oh! – there's a letter from the Captain. (*Takes letter out of his jacket pocket.*)

SYLVIA. Jerome?

GELLBURG (*terrific personal pride*). Read it. (*His purse-mouthed grin is intense.*) That's your son. General Mac-Arthur talked to him twice.

SYLVIA. Fort Sill?

GELLBURG. Oklahoma. *He's going to lecture them on artillery!* In *Fort Sill*! That's the field artillery centre. (*She looks up dumbly.*) That's like being invited to the Vatican to lecture the Pope.

SYLVIA. Imagine. (*She folds the letter and hands it back to him.*)

GELLBURG (*restraining greater resentment*). I don't understand this attitude.

SYLVIA. Why? I'm happy for him.

GELLBURG. You don't seem happy to me.

SYLVIA. I'll never get used to it. Who goes in the Army? Men who can't do anything else.

GELLBURG. I wanted people to see that a Jew doesn't have to be a lawyer or a doctor or a businessman.

SYLVIA. That's fine, but why must it be Jerome?

GELLBURG. For a Jewish boy, West Point is an honour. Without Mr Case's connections, he'd never would have gotten in. He could be the first Jewish general in the United States Army. Doesn't it mean something to be his mother?

SYLVIA (*with an edge of resentment*). Well, I said I'm glad.

GELLBURG. Don't be upset. (*Looks about impatiently.*) You know, when you get on your feet I'll help you hang the new drapes.

SYLVIA. I started to . . .

GELLBURG. But they've been here over a month.

SYLVIA. Well this happened, I'm sorry.

GELLBURG. You have to occupy yourself is all I'm saying, Sylvia, you can't give in to this.

SYLVIA (*near an outbreak*). Well I'm sorry – I'm sorry about everything!

GELLBURG. Please, don't get upset, I take it back! (*A moment; stalemate.*)

SYLVIA. I wonder what my tests show. (GELLBURG *is silent.*) That the specialist did.

GELLBURG. I went to see Dr Hyman last night.

SYLVIA. You did? Why didn't you mention it?

GELLBURG. I wanted to think over what he said.

SYLVIA. What did he say?

(*With a certain deliberateness* GELLBURG *goes over to her and gives her a kiss on the cheek. She is embarrassed and vaguely alarmed.*)

SYLVIA. Phillip! (*A little uncomprehending laugh.*)

GELLBURG. I want to change some things. About the way I've been doing.

(*He stands there for a moment perfectly still, then rolls her chair closer to the upholstered chair in which he now sits and takes her hand. She doesn't quite know what to make of his, but doesn't remove her hand.*)

SYLVIA. Well what did he say?

GELLBURG (*he pats her hand*). I'll tell you in a minute. I'm thinking about a Dodge.

SYLVIA. A Dodge?

GELLBURG. I want to teach you to drive. So you can go where you like, visit your mother in the afternoon. – I want you to be happy, Sylvia.

SYLVIA (*surprised*). Oh.

GELLBURG. We have the money, we could do a lot of things. Maybe see Washington, DC. It's supposed to be a very strong car, you know.

SYLVIA. But aren't they all black? – Dodges?

GELLBURG. Not all. I've seen a couple of green ones.

SYLVIA. You like green?

GELLBURG. It's only a colour. You'll get used to it. – Or Chicago. It's really a big city, you know.

SYLVIA. Tell me what Dr Hyman said.

GELLBURG (*gets himself set*). He thinks it could all be coming from your mind. Like a . . . a fear of some kind got into you. Psychological. (SYLVIA *is still, listening*). Are you afraid of something?

SYLVIA (*a slow shrug, a shake of her head*). . . . I don't know, I don't think so. What kind of fear, what does he mean?

GELLBURG. Well, he explains it better, but . . . like in a

22

war, people get so afraid they go blind temporarily. What they call shell-shock. But once they feel safer it goes away.

SYLVIA (*thinks about this a moment*). What about the tests the Mount Sinai men did?

GELLBURG. They can't find anything wrong with your body.

SYLVIA. But I'm numb!

GELLBURG. He claims being very frightened could be doing it. – Are you?

SYLVIA. I don't know.

GELLBURG. Personally . . . can I tell you what I think?

SYLVIA. What.

GELLBURG. I think it's this whole Nazi business.

SYLVIA. But it's in the paper – they're smashing up the Jewish stores . . . should I not read the paper? The streets are covered with broken glass!

GELLBURG. Yes, but you don't have to be constantly . . .

SYLVIA. It's ridiculous. I can't move my legs from reading a newspaper?

GELLBURG. He didn't say that; but I'm wondering if you're too involved with . . .

SYLVIA. It's ridiculous.

GELLBURG. Well, you talk to him tomorrow. (*Pause. He comes back to her and takes her hand, his need open.*) You've got to get better, Sylvia.

SYLVIA (*she sees his tortured face and tries to laugh*). What is this, am I dying or something?

GELLBURG. How can you say that?

SYLVIA. I've never seen such a look in your face.

GELLBURG. Oh no-no-no . . . I'm just worried.

SYLVIA. I don't understand what's happening . . . (*She turns away on the verge of tears.*)

GELLBURG. . . . I never realized . . . (*Sudden sharpness.*) . . . look at me, will you? (*She turns to him; he glances down*

23

at the floor.) I wouldn't know what to do without you, Sylvia, honest to God. I . . . (*Immense difficulty.*) I love you.

SYLVIA (*a dead, bewildered laugh*). What is this?

GELLBURG. You have to get better. If I'm ever doing something wrong I'll change it. Let's try to be different. All right? And you too, you've got to do what the doctors tell you.

SYLVIA. What can I do? Here I sit and they say there's nothing wrong with me.

GELLBURG. Listen . . . I think Hyman is a very smart man . . . (*He lifts her hand and kisses her knuckle; embarrassed and smiling.*) When we were talking, something came to mind; that maybe if we could sit down with him, the three of us, and maybe talk about . . . you know . . . everything.

(*Pause.*)

SYLVIA. That doesn't matter any more, Phillip.

GELLBURG (*an embarrassed grin*). How do you know? Maybe . . .

SYLVIA. It's too late for that.

GELLBURG (*once launched he is terrified*). Why? Why is it too late?

SYLVIA. I'm surprised you're still worried about it.

GELLBURG. I'm not worried, I just think about it now and then.

SYLVIA. Well, it's too late, dear, it doesn't matter any more, it hasn't for years. (*She draws back her hand.*)

(*Pause.*)

GELLBURG. . . . Well, all right. But if you wanted to I'd . . .

SYLVIA. We did talk about it, I took you to Rabbi Steiner about it twice, what good did it do?

GELLBURG. In those days I still thought it would change by itself. I was so young, I didn't understand such

24

things. It came out of nowhere and I thought it would go the same way.

SYLVIA. I'm sorry, Phillip, it didn't come out of nowhere.

(*Silent,* GELLBURG *evades her eyes.*)

SYLVIA. You regretted you got married.

GELLBURG. I didn't 'regret it' . . .

SYLVIA. You did, dear. You don't have to be ashamed of it.

(*A long silence.*)

GELLBURG. I'm going to tell you the truth – in those days I thought that if we separated I wouldn't die of it. I admit that.

SYLVIA. I always knew that.

GELLBURG. But I haven't felt that way in years now.

SYLVIA. Well, I'm here. (*Spreads her arms out, a wildly ironical look in her eyes.*) Here I am, Phillip!

GELLBURG (*offended*). The way you say that is not very . . .

SYLVIA. Not very what? I'm here; I've been here a long time.

GELLBURG (*a helpless surge of anger*). I'm trying to tell you something!

SYLVIA (*openly taunting him now*). But I said I'm here! (GELLBURG *moves about as she speaks, as though trying to find an escape or a way in.*) I'm here for my mother's sake, and Jerome's sake and everybody's sake except mine, but I'm here and here I am. And now finally you want to talk about it, now when I'm turning into an old woman? How do you want me to say it? Tell me, dear, I'll say it the way you want me to. What should I say?

GELLBURG (*insulted and guilty*). I want you to stand up.

SYLVIA. I can't stand up.

(GELLBURG *takes both her hands.*)

GELLBURG. You can. Now come on. Stand up.

SYLVIA. I can't!

GELLBURG. You can stand up, Sylvia. Now lean on me and get on your feet. (*He pulls her up; then steps aside releasing her; she collapses on the floor. He stands over her.*) What are you trying to do? (*He goes to his knees to yell into her face.*) What are you trying to do, Sylvia! (*She looks at him in terror at the mystery before her.*)

(*Blackout.*)

COMMENTARY: This scene is full of contrast between the two characters as their personalities and motivations come into open conflict. Sylvia has just got rid of her sister and has turned again to her newspapers when she is unexpectedly disturbed by Phillip's awkward arrival. Think how unusual this must be for both of them – Phillip is the kind of man who would never leave work early let alone bearing a gift, even if it is only pickles. Throughout their marriage they have kept their genuine emotions and feelings about one another bottled up. There is no easy verbal or physical familiarity between them. The doctor has told Phillip to give Sylvia 'a lot of loving' and as we see in this scene affection doesn't come easily for him. Phillip 'adores' his wife but in an almost pathological way – he needs her for his very survival. He knows how to talk business and can strike a hard bargain, but here he is inept and uneasy trying to deal with emotional and personal problems. He is full of the best intentions to cure Sylvia, but on his own terms, offering Sylvia different 'deals' to distract her. She seems weary of Phillip and gives him only the most nominal of responses: 'that's nice', 'that's sad', etc. As the scene progresses, Sylvia's mood towards Phillip changes from apparent calm indifference to outright anger and sarcasm. Notice that while Phillip is desperate to get Sylvia to walk again right here and now, she is strangely unconcerned and resigned to her plight. Sylvia is a complacent and willing invalid with an apparently insistent capacity for suffering.

26

Closer
Patrick Marber

Act 1, scene 1. Hospital. Early morning. London. 1993.

Alice (early 20s) is 'a girl from the town'. She has been working in New York as a stripper and has recently returned to London. She is an independent free spirit but refers to herself as a 'waif'. In the school of hard knocks she has learned to be tough, aggressive and purposeful. She wants everything and expects nothing. Dan (30s) is 'a man from the suburbs'. He is a frustrated writer who works for one of the London papers writing obituaries. Dan is a cynical and watchful wise guy. His life has become somewhat aimless and he drifts along from day to day barely aware of what he wants or expects from life. This scene opens the play.

(ALICE *is sitting. She is wearing a black coat. She has a rucksack by her side. Also a brown leather briefcase. She rolls down one sock. She has a cut on her leg. Quite bloody. She looks at it. She picks some strands of wool from the wound.* ALICE *looks in her rucksack and finds a box of matches. She lights a match, watches it burn, blows it out. She looks at the briefcase. Thinks. Looks around. Opens it. She searches inside. She pulls out some sandwiches in silver foil and a green apple. She opens the sandwiches and looks at the contents, smiles, puts them back. She shines the apple. She bites into it. As she starts to chew* DAN *enters. He wears a suit and an overcoat. He stops, watches her eating his apple. He is holding two hot drinks in styrofoam cups.*)

27

ALICE. Sorry. I was looking for a cigarette.

DAN. I gave up.

ALICE. Well, try harder.

(DAN *hands her a drink*.)

ALICE. Have you got to be somewhere?

DAN. Work. Didn't fancy my sandwiches?

ALICE. I don't eat fish.

DAN. Why not?

ALICE. Fish piss in the sea.

DAN. So do children.

ALICE. I don't eat children either. What's your work?

DAN. Journalism.

ALICE. What sort?

DAN. Obituaries.

ALICE. Do you like it . . . in the dying business?

DAN. *Everyone's* in the dying business.

ALICE. Dead people aren't.

(*Beat*.)

Do you think a doctor will come?

DAN. Eventually. Does it hurt?

ALICE. I'll live.

DAN. Shall I put your leg up?

ALICE. Why?

DAN. That's what people do in these situations.

ALICE. What is this 'situation'?

(*Beat*.)

DAN. Do you want me to put your leg up?

ALICE. Yes, please.

(*He lifts her leg onto a chair*.)

Who cut off your crusts?

DAN. Me.

ALICE. Did your mother cut off your crusts when you were a little boy?

DAN. I believe she did, yes.

ALICE. You should eat your crusts.

DAN. You should stop smoking.

(*Beat.*)

I've got a mobile, is there anyone you'd like to phone?

ALICE. I don't know anyone.

(*Beat.*)

Thank you for scraping me off the road.

DAN. My pleasure.

ALICE. You knight.

(DAN *looks at her.*)

DAN. You damsel.

(*Beat.*)

Why didn't you look?

ALICE. I never look where I'm going.

DAN. I looked into your eyes and then you stepped into the road.

ALICE. Then what?

DAN. You were lying on the ground, you focused on me, you said, 'Hallo, stranger.'

ALICE. What a slut.

DAN. I noticed your leg was cut.

ALICE. Did you notice my legs?

DAN. In what sense?

ALICE. In the sense of 'nice legs'?

DAN. Quite possibly.

ALICE. Then what?

DAN. The cabbie got out. He crossed himself. He said, 'Thank fuck, I thought I'd killed her.' I said, 'Let's get her to a hospital.' He hesitated, I think he thought there'd be paperwork and he'd be held responsible. So I said, with a slight sneer, 'Please, just drop us at the hospital.'

ALICE. Show me the sneer.

(DAN *sneers.*)

ALICE. Very good.

DAN. We put you in the cab and came here.

ALICE. What was I doing?

29

DAN. You were murmuring, 'I'm very sorry for all the inconvenience.' I had my arm round you, your head was on my shoulder.

ALICE. Was my head . . . 'lolling'?

DAN. That's exactly what it was doing.

(*Pause.*)

ALICE. You have the saddest looking bun I've ever seen. Can I have it?

(DAN *opens his briefcase.*)

ALICE. You'll be late for work.

DAN. Are you saying you want me to go?

ALICE. No.

(*She puts her hand in the briefcase.*)

DAN. You can have half.

(*She removes the bun, tears it in two and begins to eat.*)
Why were you at Blackfriars Bridge?

ALICE. I'd been dancing at a club near Smithfield. I went for a walk. I went to see the meat being unloaded.

DAN. The carcasses?

ALICE. Yes.

DAN. Why?

ALICE. Because they're repulsive. Then I found a tiny park . . . it's a graveyard too. Postman's Park. Do you know it?

(DAN *shakes his head.*)

ALICE. There's a memorial to ordinary people who died saving the lives of others. It's most curious. Then I decided to go to Borough . . . so I went to Blackfriars Bridge to cross the river.

(*Pause.* DAN *offers her the other half of the bun.*)

ALICE. Are you sure?

DAN. Yeah, it's yesterday's sad bun.

(*Beat.*)
That park . . . it's near here?

(ALICE *nods.*)

DAN. Is there a statue?

ALICE. A Minotaur.

DAN. I do know it . . . we sat there . . . (my mother's dead) . . . my father and I sat there the afternoon she died. She died here actually . . . she was a smoker. My father . . . ate . . . an egg sandwich . . . I remember his hands shaking with grief . . . pieces of egg falling onto the grass . . . butter on his top lip . . . but I don't remember . . . a memorial. (*Pause.*)

ALICE. Is your father still alive?

DAN. Just. He's in a home.

ALICE. How did you end up writing obituaries? What did you really want to be?

(*Pause.*)

DAN. Oh . . . I had dreams of being a writer but I had no voice – no talent. So . . . I ended up in the 'Siberia' of journalism.

ALICE. Tell me what you do. I want to imagine you in . . . Siberia.

DAN. Really?

ALICE. Yes.

DAN. Well . . . we call it 'the obits page'. There's three of us; me, Harry and Graham. The first thing someone will say (usually Graham) is 'Who's on the slab?' Meaning did anyone important die overnight. Are you sure you want to know?

ALICE. Yes.

DAN. If someone did die we go to the 'deep freeze' which is a computer containing all the obituaries and we'll find the dead person's life.

ALICE. People's obituaries are already written when they're still alive?

DAN. Mmhmm. If no one important has died then Harry – he's the editor – decides who we lead with and we check facts, make calls, polish the prose. Some days I might be

31

asked to deal with the widows or widowers. They try to persuade us to run an obituary of their husbands or wives. They feel we're dishonouring their loved ones if we don't . . . but . . . most of them are . . . well, there isn't the space. At six we stand round the computer and read the next day's page, make final changes, put in a few euphemisms to amuse ourselves . . .

ALICE. Such as?

DAN. 'He was a clubbable fellow', meaning he was an alcoholic. 'He valued his privacy' – gay. 'He enjoyed his privacy' – raging queen. 'She was a convivial hostess' –

ALICE. A pissed old slapper?

DAN. Exactly.

(*Pause. ALICE strokes DAN's face. He is surprised but not unwilling.*)

ALICE. And what would your euphemism be . . .

DAN. For me?

ALICE. Mmm.

DAN. He was . . . 'reserved'.

ALICE. A lonely old bastard?

DAN. Perhaps.

ALICE. And me?

DAN. You were . . . 'disarming'.

(*Beat.*)

ALICE. How did you get this job?

DAN. They ask you to write your own obituary . . . and . . . if it amuses, you're in.

(*They are close, looking at each other.*)

COMMENTARY: In this quintessential urban play Marber explores the twin imperatives of sexual jealousy and sexual desire. The accident which randomly throws Dan and Alice together acts as a catalyst for both of them to become 'closer'. Despite the potentially inauspicious beginning, there seems to be a mutual

32

interest between them. Dan is aware that there was a frisson of attraction from the moment he made eye contact with Alice just before the accident. A wary curiosity informs their bantering exchange; they are testing and teasing each other. Alice is impulsive and confrontational and at times she sounds like a naive but articulate child, trying to provoke a reaction. She likes to think she is in control of her destiny and her sexuality, 'I know what men want . . . Men want a girl who looks like a boy. They want to protect her but she must be a survivor. And she must come . . . like a train . . . but with elegance.' Dan, although more circumspect and conventional, seems charmed by her flirtatious cheekiness and gamely goes along with Alice's baiting. Dan appears slightly goofy, impulsive and in need of mothering. Throughout the play Alice retains an enigmatic quality, no matter how 'close' she gets to people she never fully reveals herself. By the end of the play it turns out that even her name is a fiction.

Dog Opera
Constance Congdon

Act 1. Jones Beach on Long Island. New York. The present.

Madeline Newell (35 or so) is single and works as a librarian in a New York City elementary school. Peter Szczepanek (35 or so) is single, gay and works in an office. They have been best friends and confidants for the past twenty-five years; when they were both still at school Madeline had an abortion and Pete was there to hold her hand. They now see one another regularly and phone at least once a day. They are hip, urban and desperately seeking romance and relationships. In this scene they 'are semi-reclining in aluminum chaises on a public beach, under a beach umbrella. They are wearing T-shirts, hats, sunglasses and towels over their thighs. The are sharing a can of Diet Coke.'

PETE. There's just one thing . . .
MADELINE. What?
PETE. One thing I'm worried about.
MADELINE. What?
PETE. Will guys think I'm a transsexual?
MADELINE. You're too hairy.
PETE. I could be in transition.
MADELINE. If you'd take off that towel –
PETE. And let the world see my thighs?
I don't think so.
MADELINE. *Your* thighs? Puh-leeze.
PETE. There's nothing wrong with your thighs.
MADELINE. If Jacques Cousteau were here, I'd be on PBS. Okay?
(Sees a guy.) Oh man.

34

PETE. Where?

MADELINE. At three o'clock.

PETE. Now – wait a minute. Where is midnight?

MADELINE. Straight ahead.

PETE. And six is back here.

MADELINE. You're going to miss him.

PETE. Where?

MADELINE. I'm not pointing. Forget it.

PETE (*spying the guy*). Oh, wait a minute. Blue Speedos?

MADELINE. Grey.

PETE. If you're quibbling about the color, how great can this guy be?

MADELINE. You missed him.

PETE (*sees another guy*). Whoa, doggies.

MADELINE. What is this? Jed Clampett cruises Jones Beach?

PETE. Lord have mercy.

MADELINE (*sees this guy*). Oh my.

PETE. Ohhhh. Ohhhhh. Mama.

MADELINE. A basket worthy of Carmen Miranda's head.

PETE. She'll have to fight me for him.

MADELINE. Buns.

PETE (*they take him in*). Buns.

MADELINE. Gay.

PETE. Straight.
(*Reconsidering.*) Straight.

MADELINE. Gay.

PETE. No way.

MADELINE. Invite him over.
If I fall in love with him – he's gay.

PETE. If I fall in love with him – he's straight.
(*Weakly.*) Oh, sir? Sir? Can you come over here and ruin our lives?

MADELINE. Oh, please, it's been at least two weeks.

PETE. Oh my God.

MADELINE. What?

PETE. He's looking at us.

MADELINE. Oh jeez.

PETE. I'm going to take off my towel.

MADELINE. That should do it.

PETE. What's that supposed to mean?

MADELINE. Peter, take off the towel.

(PETE *takes his towel off – he's wearing a long pair of black bathing trunks*.)

MADELINE. Those *are* fetching.

PETE. He's coming over, Madeline!

Oh fuck.

MADELINE. Will you relax?

PETE. He's looking at me.

MADELINE. I knew he was gay. He's motioning . . .

PETE. I've attracted a deaf-mute.

It'll be like *Children of a Lesser God*.

Oh my God! I'm Bill Hurt! (*To guy*.) What?

Oh no, I don't have any – sorry! I quit six months ago.

(PETE *watches guy exit*.) But I'd be glad to make you one if you bring me the tobacco! (*Guy is gone*.) Or just bring me your seeds and we'll grow it together.

Or if you have a gun, I'd be glad to shoot myself in the other foot. (PETE *sits down*.) I'm sure he appreciated the lecture on quitting smoking.

MADELINE. It wasn't a lecture.

It was a comment.

PETE. He was gay, Madeline.

And he almost talked to me until I turned into Bobby Bizarro.

MADELINE. Pete – he was straight.

PETE. How do you know?

MADELINE. If he were gay, he would have talked to me, too.

PETE. You're right.

I wasn't just rejected.

MADELINE. You weren't just rejected.

PETE. I was asked for a cigarette.

And I didn't have any.

MADELINE. That simple. (*Long beat.*) I was rejected. He didn't even talk to me.

I don't know – maybe the towel makes me look fatter.

PETE. Take it off.

MADELINE. When pigs fly. (*Beat.*) When pigs fly, maybe I'll join the air force – at last, a suit that fits me.

PETE. Stop it.

I like that black thing you bought.

MADELINE. Which black thing? All my clothes are black.

PETE. The dressy suit thing.

MADELINE. Oh, my memorial outfit?

PETE. I guess so.

MADELINE. It's ten years old!

I bought it for . . . Barry.

PETE. Barry.

Barry's memorial.

That's an old suit.

MADELINE. Too old.

Burn it.

Take it out and burn it.

I need a new suit, Peter.

PETE. Me, too.

Hey! Hey, hey, hey!

What are we doin'?

MADELINE. We are cruisin'.

We are strategically placed just to the left of Field Six at Jones Beach, so the pickin's are great.

PETE. And the livin' is easy.

MADELINE. Straight men to the left of me.

PETE. Gay men to the right of me.

MADELINE. Into the valley of . . . *life*
Rode the six hundred.

PETE. And that's why there are no cute guys –
Six hundred hunky light brigade officers rode up –

MADELINE. And took the cute ones – (*Sees a guy.*)
– wait a minute. Nine o'clock. Approaching –

PETE. Now, where's nine again?

MADELINE (*showing him quickly*). Noon. Three. Six.
Nine.

PETE (*sees him*). Very attractive black man?

MADELINE. Red Speedos.

PETE. Oh my God.
Remind me to make an offering to the god of nylon.

MADELINE. All synthetic fibers aren't bad. (*They watch
him.*)

PETE. Well, that made my afternoon.

MADELINE. Yeah. (*Still watching as he disappears down
the beach.*)

PETE. Gay? Straight?

MADELINE. Beautiful.

COMMENTARY: *Dog Opera* humorously examines the emotionally intimate friendship between a gay man and a straight
woman. This scene requires careful playing to achieve a balance
between the flip comedy and the characters' genuine anxiety.
Madeline and Pete are 'cruisin' the beach without moving a
muscle. It is vital to create the world of the beach for your
audience; the warm sun, the relaxed indolence, the sense of the
other people and especially the 'cute guys'. The clock device
should help you to animate and people the beach. Madeline and
Pete's voyeurism gives the scene its unique comic flavour. The

two friends have an easy familiarity and a camaraderie which is never threatened by rivalry. Notice how they both suffer from lack of confidence and indulge in bouts of comic self-deprecation. They are passing the time, assessing the action and desperately trying to judge the sexuality of all the 'beautiful' men.

The Heidi Chronicles
Wendy Wasserstein

Act 1, scene 1. A high-school gym in Chicago, with folding chairs, streamers and a table with a punch bowl. 1965.

Heidi Holland (16) is wearing a traditional A-line dress. She is a hard-working student at the elite Miss Crain's school where she edits the school newspaper. She has come to this high-school dance with her best friend, Susan, who is eager to find a dance partner, whereas Heidi prefers sitting and watching on the sidelines. When she is approached by a boy she gives him a sardonic cold shoulder. Peter (16) is wearing a St Mark's school blazer. He is also a highly motivated, articulate and academic student. As the scene begins Susan has just left Heidi who 'sits on a chair, takes out a book, reads it for a moment, then puts it on her lap as she stares out. "Play with fire" is played. Peter . . . approaches. She smiles and looks down.'

PETER. You must be very bright.
HEIDI. Excuse me?
PETER. You look so bored you must be very bright.
HEIDI. I'm sorry?
PETER. Don't be sorry. I appreciate bored people. Bored, depressed, anxious. These are the qualities I look for in a woman. Your lady friend is dancing with the gentleman who looks like Bobby Kennedy. I find men who smoke and twist at the same time so dreary.
HEIDI. Not worth the coordination, really.
PETER. Do you have any?
HEIDI. I can sit and read at the same time.
PETER. What book is that?
HEIDI. *Death Be Not Proud.*

PETER. Of course.

HEIDI. A favorite of mine at dances.

PETER. I was drawn to you from the moment I saw you shielding that unfortunate wench rolling up her garments in the tempest.

HEIDI. I'm sorry.

PETER. Please. Don't apologize for being the most attractive woman on this cruise.

HEIDI. Cruise?

PETER. She docks tonight in Portsmouth. And then farewell to the *Queen Mary*. Forever to harbor in Long Beach, California. *C'est triste, n'est pas?*

HEIDI. *Ce n'est pas bon.*

PETER (*excitedly*). Our tragic paths were meant to cross. I leave tomorrow for the sanatorium in Zurich. (*Coughs.*)

HEIDI. How odd! I'm going to the sanatorium in Milan. (*Coughs. He offers her his handkerchief. She refuses.*)

PETER. My parents are heartbroken. They thought I was entering Williams College in the fall.

HEIDI. My parents put down a deposit at Vassar.

PETER. We've only this night together. I'm Peter, a small noise from Winnetka. I tried to pick out your name . . . Amanda, Lady Clara, Estelle . . .

HEIDI. It's . . .

PETER. No, don't tell me. I want to remember you as you are. Beside me in the moonlight, the stars above us . . .

HEIDI. The sea below us.

PETER. Glenn Miller and the orchestra. It's all so peaceful.

HEIDI. Mmmmmm. Quite peaceful.

(*'The Shoop Shoop Song' is heard again.*)

PETER. The twist-and-smokers are heaving themselves on their lady friends. This must be the final song. Would you do me the honor of one dance?

41

HEIDI. Certainly.

PETER. Ahhh! 'The Shoop Shoop Song'. Baroque but fragile.

HEIDI. Melodic but atonal.

PETER. Will you marry me?

HEIDI. I covet my independence.

PETER. Perhaps when you leave the sanatorium, you'll think otherwise. I want to know you all my life. If we can't marry, let's be great friends.

HEIDI. I will keep your punch cup, as a memento, beside my pillow.

PETER. Well, shall we hully-gully, baby?

HEIDI. Really, I . . .

PETER. Don't worry, I'll teach you.

(*He begins to do a form of shimmy line dance. Holding HEIDI's hand, he instructs her. The dance is somewhat interpretive and becomes a minuet. They sing as they dance together.*)

PETER.

How 'bout the way he acts?

HEIDI.

Oh, noooo, that's not the way.

PETER.

And you're not listenin' to all I say.

If you wanna know if he loves you so . . .

(*Takes HEIDI'S waist and dips her.*)

PETER.

It's in his kiss.

HEIDI & PETER.

Oh, yeah! It's in his kiss!

(*They continue to dance as the lights fade.*)

COMMENTARY: This play follows the progress of American baby-boomer Heidi Holland from high school to early middle age. Heidi really doesn't want to be at this party with its old-fashioned courtship rituals. She obviously planned on being a party pooper since she brought a book along with her. She has an extremely ironic sensibility which gets in the way of her enjoying the party to the full. That is until Peter comes along whose own sardonic and theatrical attitudes seem to be perfectly in tune with Heidi's. His charm and ironic wit quickly break down her reserve and together they create a hammy parody of B-movie romantic dialogue. They are both slightly unusual, eccentric and, as it turns out, soulmates. They remain friends but never become lovers. The play reveals that fifteen years later Peter, much to Heidi's surprise and disappointment, is a 'liberal-homosexual pediatrician'.

The Lodger
Simon Burke

Scene 1. A bed-sitting room in Wise's house. A small, dreary suburban town somewhere north of King's Cross.

Andrew Wise (mid 40s) has 'a calm exterior – phlegmatic with a slow burn. He is still attractive, in a rugged and physical sort of way, but obviously has no interest in fashion.' Lois ('lost somewhere in her thirties but perhaps looks older') is 'a beautiful woman who has, perhaps, had more than her share of troubles. She is dressed smartly, but not fashionably, for business.' The play begins with this scene. Wise 'is shy and ill at ease as he turns to hold the door open' for Lois.

WISE. This is the room. Obviously.
(*His accent is Southern working-middle class. LOIS looks round. It is a poor little room, unloved and unlit. The fixtures and fittings are as cheap as may be procured anywhere and there are as few of them as possible.*)
LOIS. And thirty quid a week, yeah?
WISE. Er, yes. If er . . . if that's all right . . .
(*She casts a dubious eye over the fittings.*)
LOIS. Well, it seems a pretty shit deal for living here but, what the hell, I need the money.
(*He stares at her blankly. She smiles, which softens her careworn features.*)
It was a joke.
(*WISE nods seriously as she moves over to test the bed for squeaks. She sits down on it and pulls out a pack of cigarettes. Her accent betrays an education and a professional upbringing.*)

LOIS. Do you smoke?

WISE. No.

LOIS. Do you mind if I have one?

(*She doesn't wait for an answer.* WISE *does mind, but says nothing about it.*)

WISE. You're not from round here then?

LOIS. No.

WISE. From London?

LOIS. Yeah.

WISE. You working up here?

LOIS. For a bit.

WISE. So you wouldn't be here long?

LOIS. Hard to say. Does the thirty quid include the questions?

WISE. Well, obviously, if you're going to be living here, I want to know a bit about you.

LOIS. I want a room, not a relationship.

WISE. It's not that –

LOIS. I like my privacy.

(*He backs off, chastened.*)

WISE. Sorry – I haven't done this before.

LOIS. I have. It's easy: I give you money. You give me key.

WISE. Right. Yes.

LOIS. Who else lives here then?

WISE. Just me at the moment.

LOIS. So you're not married?

WISE. No.

LOIS. You've got a wedding ring.

(WISE *looks at his ring finger, then puts his hands in his pockets.*)

How come you're renting the room out?

WISE. Well, the money'll be useful. Obviously.

LOIS. You don't work then? As such.

WISE. Yes, no, I do, but the mortgage and everything . . .

45

I bought at the top of the market. It's hard to sell . . .
Things have become a bit tight recently . . . you know . . .
(*She nods sympathetically as he trails off. She sits on the bed,
apparently relaxed and self-possessed, but the way she smokes
hungrily gives a hint at something more brittle beneath the
surface, even desperate. She has a distinct but understated
sexual allure. She is aware of her body and knows how to use it.
She is not using it on* WISE.)

LOIS. So, what do you do then?

WISE. Oh I work in security . . . Shift work . . . It varies.
And you?

LOIS. What's it matter what I do? I want a room, not a
job.

(*She looks at him blankly, puzzled. He's flustered, on the back
foot.*)

WISE. Well, I'm asking what you do, just, because, to be
sure you can afford the rent. That's all . . .

LOIS. If I couldn't afford the rent, why would I come
here? I mean, you'd ask me for the rent, and I wouldn't
have it and you'd throw me out and I'd have nowhere to
live. Why would I do that?

(WISE *has to laugh, though not with much humour. She
relents*:)

All right. I'm a researcher. For a market research company.

WISE. Sounds interesting.

LOIS. It's a job. It's not *supposed* to be interesting. I work
when I like, choose my own times. It's OK.

WISE. I'm surprised they don't put you up in a hotel . . .

(*She considers him coolly.*)

LOIS. OK, I'll be honest: they give me an allowance for a
hotel, but if I can get cheaper accommodation, I can keep
the change, right? We're not supposed to, but no one
minds.

WISE. Researching what?

(*The faintest flicker of hesitation, which she covers by blowing a smoke ring. WISE opens a window.*)

LOIS. Social trends. I'm sorry, I'm not supposed to tell people the details. Bit pathetic, but there you are. It's a government contract. There. Feel better now?

WISE. No offence.

LOIS. Are you saying, you don't want anything to do with people on the dole, is what you're hinting?

WISE. No, not particularly –

LOIS. A lot of landlords don't want unemployed people.

WISE. No . . . Obviously.

LOIS. In case their rent payments go on record.

(*He frowns, then gets her meaning.*)

WISE. There's nothing below board about this.

LOIS. But you'd prefer cash?

(*He looks at her uncertainly. She smiles.*)

Don't worry, I'm not from the Inland Revenue.

WISE. I'm not worried. This is all perfectly kosher.

LOIS. Sure, sure, I just like to know who I'm dealing with, that's all, nothing personal – just business.

WISE. Obviously. Business.

LOIS. OK. I'll take it. I'll give you cash in advance, two weeks' if you want.

(*She rummages through her shoulder bag.*)

WISE. Oh, fine. OK. Ah, do you have references?

LOIS. References?

(*She looks up at him, half amused, half irritated.*)

WISE. Yes . . . Bank, or employer . . . Or something . . .

LOIS. I'm sorry, I've forgotten your name –

WISE. Wise. Andrew Wise.

LOIS. OK, Andrew, are you going to give *me* references? Are you going to give me, for example, letters from two people who've lived here?

WISE. What?

LOIS. I mean, if anyone needs references, it's me that

needs references not you, especially as I'm a girl. I mean I don't know *anything* about you. I don't even know this is actually your house. Do I? You could be any one.

WISE. This is silly.

LOIS. Is it? I suppose women don't get raped any more. What a *relief*.

WISE. No, obviously, I'm sorry, I didn't mean that . . .

LOIS. OK, Andrew, what are you worried about? I mean, am I likely to ruin your career? Destroy your life as you know it? You think that's likely? Kill you maybe?

WISE. No, no. It's just that it's *normal*, you know, references. It's what tenants give landlords.

LOIS. Come on I mean you own this room, you own this house, so you say, you can decide whether to let me live here or not on the vaguest whim, you can beat me up and throw me out at a second's notice and me I have to have a strange man sleeping next door after what I've been through it seems to me I'm the one that needs protection, fucking references is what it seems I need. Me . . .

WISE. I'm sorry. I didn't mean to upset you.

LOIS. That's OK. You didn't . . . It's just a question of trust.

WISE. Look, I'm sorry . . . it's just (*Groping for an excuse.*) there's someone else coming to look at the room.

(*She looks round at him.*)

LOIS. Is there? You just made that up, didn't you?

WISE (*flustered*). No, no . . . I didn't.

LOIS. OK, who's coming then?

(WISE *hesitates. She runs her hands through her hair; she suddenly looks exhausted.*)

It's *such* a bad lie. I've come a long way and I'm shattered and I think I deserve a much better one.

WISE. Look –

LOIS. Excuse me, wait a minute. I can't believe my ears – are you saying, is someone actually saying, I'm not good

48

enough to live here? *Here?* What sort of person isn't good
enough to live *here?*

WISE. Thanks for coming. I hope you find somewhere
you like. Suitable.

(*She realises he is serious and stares at him, stunned.*)

LOIS. Look, Andrew, I mean, look at this place. Look at
it. Who're you expecting to rent this? I mean, *what?* You
think maybe Japanese businessmen looking for a pied-à-
terre maybe, or maybe like Fergie and her mates looking
for a little hideaway, I mean what sort of person you
expect here? I mean, I have clothes. I *wash.* Which seems
to me more than you can reasonably expect for this room,
is what seems to me. I even have money. Cash.

(WISE *clearly hates a row.*)

I've never heard such a fuss about a thirty-quid room
before.

WISE. Well, it's just, I live here too. It's not just business.
Exactly.

(*Her temper subsides . . . She takes a deep breath.*)

LOIS. Sure, OK. I'm sorry. Look, I'm tired and wet and
bad-tempered and I've nowhere else to go and it's late and
it's raining. This is OK and I want to stay. Here, take the
money.

(*She holds it towards him, but he doesn't take it.*)

WISE. I'm sorry. I don't think this is going to work out.

LOIS. You're thinking, maybe you and me, we've maybe
got off on the wrong foot, is what you're thinking yeah?

WISE (*incredulous*). Well, maybe.

LOIS. It's OK, I don't hold grudges. (*She smiles.*) And I
won't need a deposit.

(*He returns her smile nervously.*)

WISE. Look, Miss –

LOIS. Lois.

WISE. I'm sorry . . .

49

(*He sighs. A moment. Her face crumples. She starts to weep. He simply can't cope with this.*)

LOIS. Where do you want me to go?

WISE. I don't know . . . Where did you come from?

LOIS. A shitty bed and breakfast by the station. It was horrible.

WISE. I'm sorry . . . look . . . Lois . . . Please . . .

LOIS. You want me to go back *there*?

WISE. No, no – look . . . it's just . . .

(*He trails off miserably. She looks up at him hopefully with tearful, mascara-smudged eyes.*)

LOIS (*sniff*). Or do you want me to go to the Inland Revenue?

WISE. What?

(*She dries her eyes miserably. A moment. He can't believe his ears. She smiles tearfully up at him.*)

LOIS. Please can't I stay?

(*His mouth hangs open a second.*)

WISE. I've got nothing to hide.

LOIS. No, of course. It's just a question of trust.

(*She puts the money on the bedside table. He looks at it, then her, unable to talk. Then the phone rings. As if in a dream, he goes to answer it.*)

WISE. Hello . . . No, er . . . the room . . . yes . . .

(*The moment hangs and grows with his physical discomfort.*)

No . . . I'm afraid it's just been taken. Thank you.

(*He puts the phone down.*)

(*Blackout.*)

COMMENTARY: This play portrays the angst of lonely people driven to desperation. All the characters conceal their motives and intentions. Wise claims to be a security guard; Lois claims to be in market research. Both, of course, are lying and although the actors must be aware of this they should be very careful how they use this knowledge. It must inform the evasive way the characters behave; both of them are hiding their true identities for a reason. She is tired and bolshy; he is shy and uncertain of what he is doing. They have both been injured emotionally and physically in the past and they are extremely wary and suspicious of new people. They ruthlessly interrogate each other with limited success. Notice how each question is met with a deflected evasion. The more he probes the more suspicious she in turn becomes. Wise is really a Detective Constable in the CID. He is lonely and desperate since his wife left him and has resorted, unsuccessfully, to a computer dating agency. Lois is a prostitute with a drug habit who has fled London and her violent pimp. She has come to Wise's house as a temporary refuge. How desperate is she? Why does Wise, after so much resistance, finally give in?

The Pitchfork Disney
Philip Ridley

'Night. A dimly lit room in the East End of London: front door with many bolts . . . Everything old and colourless.'

Presley and Haley Stray are twenty-eight-year-old twins. 'Presley is dressed in dirty pyjamas, vest, frayed cardigan and slippers. He is unshaven, hair unevenly hacked very short, teeth discoloured, skin pale, dark rings beneath bloodshot eyes.' Haley 'is wearing an old nightdress beneath a man's frayed dressing gown. Her hair is longer, but still unevenly cut. Teeth and complexion the same as Presley's.' The twins have lived together all their lives. They are both chocoholics; their addiction is so extreme that they survive solely on a diet of chocolate. When they were eighteen years old their parents mysteriously 'disappeared', and since then their relationship has become increasingly obsessive; they are both still virgins. The only bequest from their parents was a supply of medicine and tranquilisers that they ration between themselves. Always in a state of terror and dread, they experience the world as a living nightmare. Macabre and bizarre fantasy defines their existence. Although they are in their late twenties they regress and behave like children: it is as if the clock stopped for them when they were ten years old. They live hermetically together in a fortified home, shunning all contact with the outside. Presley dominates their relationship, intimidating Haley by rationing their parents' leftover drugs to keep her docile. Presley is the historian of the uniquely bizarre version of their happy, golden childhood. Haley relies on Presley to recount key episodes for her. As the play opens, Haley 'is sitting at the table. She is fiddling with a tiny piece of chocolate wrapping paper.' Presley 'is staring into the darkness outside'.

(Sounds of dogs howling outside. HALEY flinches, looks at PRESLEY anxiously. PRESLEY looks at her. The dogs continue howling. Pause. Sound of dogs fades. PRESLEY looks out of the window. HALEY continues to look anxious.)

HALEY. Describe it.

PRESLEY. Again?

HALEY. Just once more, Presley.

PRESLEY *(sighing)*. You said that last time.

HALEY. Did I? I don't remember.

PRESLEY. You know your trouble, Haley? You break your promises. You say one thing but you mean another. You don't play fair. Sometimes I think you're nothing but a . . .

HALEY *(interrupting)*. What?

PRESLEY. Oh, nothing.

HALEY. Go on. Say it.

PRESLEY. Well, a cheat.

HALEY. Don't call me that. It's not fair. Not after what happened this morning.

PRESLEY. What do you mean?

HALEY. With the shopping, I mean.

PRESLEY. What about it?

HALEY. The chocolate, Presley. I'm talking about the chocolate. You bought fruit and nut.

PRESLEY. So?

HALEY. You know I don't like fruit and nut. You know it makes me sick. The nut gets caught between my teeth and the raisins taste like bits of skin.

PRESLEY. How do you know what skin tastes like?

HALEY. I can use my imagination.

PRESLEY. Well, you used to like fruit and nut.

HALEY. I've never liked fruit and nut. *You* like fruit and nut. You know my favourite is orange chocolate . . .

PRESLEY *(interrupting)*. I didn't just buy fruit and nut. I bought other things as well.

HALEY. What other things?

PRESLEY. Lots of things.

HALEY. You didn't tell me.

PRESLEY (*sighing*). I did, Haley.

HALEY. Well, I must have forgotten. Where are they?

PRESLEY. In the drawer.

(*HALEY goes to drawer in sideboard. She opens it, discovers many bars of different chocolate. The chocolate is in bright wrapping paper.*)

HALEY. Oh, Presley . . . I can see orange chocolate.

(*She takes chocolate bars to the table. Spreads them over the surface as if they're jewels.*)

HALEY. Come and eat, Presley.

PRESLEY. Don't want to.

HALEY. You're sulking now.

PRESLEY. You shouldn't accuse me of just buying fruit and nut.

HALEY. I'm sorry. It's just that I saw you eating a bar earlier. I assumed that's all there was. I can see now . . . there's a big selection . . . Come on. (*Picks up a bar of fruit and nut and waves it temptingly in the air.*) Fruit and nut. Fruit and nut.

(*PRESLEY and HALEY sit at the table and begin to eat chocolate.*)

PRESLEY. There's more chocolate than ever in the shops now, Haley. You go in and it sparkles like treasure. Flaky chocolate, mint chocolate, crispy chocolate . . .

HALEY (*overlapping*). . . . Bubbly chocolate . . .

PRESLEY (*overlapping*). . . . Wafer chocolate . . .

HALEY (*overlapping*). . . . Chocolate with cream in . . .

PRESLEY (*overlapping*). . . . Chocolate with nuts in . . .

HALEY (*overlapping*). . . . Which I don't like.

PRESLEY (*overlapping*). . . . Which you don't like. All sorts of chocolate in all sorts of paper.

(*HALEY is sorting through the pile for another bar of orange chocolate.*)

PRESLEY. . . . There's coffee chocolate and mint chocolate and strawberry chocolate and . . .

HALEY (*giving up her search*). Well, that's typical.

PRESLEY. What?

HALEY. You bought . . . (*Sorting through the pile of chocolate and counting.*) . . . one, two, three, four, plus the one you're eating, plus the one this morning, that's six bars of fruit and nut and only one bar of orange.

PRESLEY (*staring, chocolate in mouth*). I'm sorry. I must have got carried away.

HALEY. You did it on purpose.

PRESLEY. There's other things, Haley. Look! Flaky chocolate and bubbly chocolate and crispy rice chocolate . . .

HALEY (*firmly*). My favourite is orange chocolate. (*Pause.*) This is just like you, Presley. Sometimes you're so . . .

PRESLEY (*interrupting*). What?

HALEY. Oh, nothing.

PRESLEY. Go on. Say it.

HALEY. Well, selfish.

PRESLEY. Don't call me that. It's not fair. Not after what *you* did this morning.

HALEY. What did I do?

PRESLEY. About going out to get the shopping in the first place.

HALEY. What about it?

PRESLEY. You know it was your turn.

HALEY. Was not.

PRESLEY. Was!

HALEY. Wasn't!

PRESLEY. Was!

HALEY. Wasn't!

PRESLEY. Was! Was! Was!

HALEY. How? How was it my turn?

PRESLEY. Because I went yesterday. That's how.

HALEY. No you didn't.

PRESLEY. Yes I did. You know I did. I bought the milk and the bread. They were in a brown paper bag. I put them on the table. You were sitting where you're sitting now. You said, 'Didn't you buy any biscuits?' And I said, 'Yes.' I gave them to you. They were in a blue packet. I made you a cup of tea and you dunked the biscuits in the tea. Afterwards, I put the milk and what was left of the biscuits in the fridge.

HALEY. Biscuits? In the fridge?

PRESLEY. That's right.

HALEY. In a blue packet?

PRESLEY. Yes.

HALEY. A blue packet with yellow and red stripes?

PRESLEY. Yes.

HALEY. That means they're orange chocolate biscuits, Presley.

PRESLEY. I know.

HALEY. Well, why didn't you tell me? I've felt like a biscuit all day.

PRESLEY. But you saw me put them in the fridge.

HALEY. I forgot. You know I need reminding. If you make me a cup of tea and don't offer me a biscuit, then I assume all the biscuits have gone. I don't think you're hiding them from me.

PRESLEY. I wasn't hiding them . . .

HALEY (*standing*). Yes you were! You were going to wait for me to take my tablet, then eat them all yourself. (*Starts to make her way to the fridge.*)

PRESLEY. But I don't even like the biscuits. I got them for you. You're just trying to change the subject.

HALEY (*stopping in her tracks*). From what?

PRESLEY. From why you said it wasn't your turn to get the shopping when you know full well it was.

56

HALEY (*returning to the table*). Don't blame me. You remember what happened last time I went to the shops. It was terrible. I was so scared. I came back crying and shaking. My clothes were torn and wet. There was blood on my legs. You wiped it away with a tissue. I was crying so much I couldn't breathe properly. You remember that, Presley? I was hysterical. Wasn't I? Hysterical?

PRESLEY (*softly*). I suppose so.

HALEY. You were so nice. You put your arms round me and let me suck the dummy. You remember that?

PRESLEY. Yes.

COMMENTARY: Haley and Presley are like children in a fairy tale: innocents threatened by an evil (in this case nuclear) world. The siblings act like half-crazed, abandoned children. Living in such claustrophobic squalor they petulantly manipulate and menace each other. The minutiae of daily life become cause for constant conflict. Notice how childlike their language and behaviour are: they squabble, sulk and whine like jealous toddlers on the verge of terrible tantrums. Yet being adults they have the stamina to keep their squabbles going and growing. They live in utter fear of the unknown and the world outside. A trip to the shops is a perilous journey into the wild. The childhood trauma they appear to have suffered is never made entirely clear. Their only refuge is with each other. Notice how important visual things are to both twins; they relish the colours, textures and vividness of everything around them. Even mundane chocolate bars become technicolour jewels in their 'colourless' world. Their fixation with chocolate has mutated into an all-consuming sensual fetish. However, it is a challenge for the actors to convince the audience that the twins are real and not merely comic players in a surreal nightmare.

(NB A later scene from this play can be found on page 142 of this volume.)

Raised in Captivity
Nicky Silver

Act 1, scene 3. The Dixons' living room. It is the middle of the night.

Bernadette (early 30s) and Kip Dixon (mid 30s) have been married for eight years. Kip is a dentist but hates teeth. He comes from a very poor background. After graduating from high school he robbed a man on the subway and used his credit cards to buy tickets to fly to Europe. He panhandled until he got a job as a guide at the 'depressing' Anne Frank House in Amsterdam. This was where he first met Bernadette who was on a European tour with her domineering mother. Bernadette is highly strung and often on the verge of tears: her twin brother, Sebastian, thinks she is 'completely insane'. As she is all too aware, her life has an aimless quality. She spends her time shopping, while her contemporaries pursue high-flying careers. She is obsessed with her weight and has a 'neurotic relationship with food'. Bernadette's mother recently died in a freak accident and this scene occurs the night after the funeral. 'Kip is looking out the window. After a moment Bernadette enters wearing a bathrobe.'

BERNADETTE. Kip?

KIP. Did I wake you?

BERNADETTE. What are you doing?

KIP. It's a beautiful night. The clouds have passed.

BERNADETTE. I woke up and the bed was empty. I didn't know where you were.

KIP. I didn't mean to wake you.

BERNADETTE. I got scared.

KIP. Come look at this.

BERNADETTE. Is something out there?

KIP. Come here.

BERNADETTE. I'm tired. It's been a very long, trying day.

KIP (*turning away*). Then go to bed.

BERNADETTE. Are you coming?

KIP. No.

BERNADETTE. What are you looking at? (*She goes to the window.*)

KIP. The moon.

BERNADETTE. The moon? The moon, Kip? You're looking at the moon?

KIP. Isn't it beautiful?

BERNADETTE. It looks dirty.

KIP. What would you call that color?

BERNADETTE (*exasperated*). White?

KIP. No, I don't think so. It's definitely not white.

BERNADETTE. Who cares?

KIP. Ecru, maybe. Or eggshell!

BERNADETTE. It's a big, dirty circle in the sky. Come back to bed.

KIP. Something happened today!

BERNADETTE. It's not that I'm not fascinated –

KIP. Listen to me.

BERNADETTE. Although, I'm not.

KIP. Do you realize that I never knew anyone who died before? It's true. My whole life, I never knew anyone who died. Isn't that startling?

BERNADETTE. I don't understand!

KIP. Did you know you're going to die? I didn't! I mean I had the information, tucked away in some remote corner of my brain, but seeing your mother, lifeless, still – seeing someone I didn't even like as an object made my own death a very tangible entity.

59

BERNADETTE. Everyone's going to die! Everyone born will die.

That's a very bleak point of view, Bernadette.

BERNADETTE. Life is finite. Thank God.

KIP (*with great importance*). I don't want to be a dentist.

BERNADETTE (*stunned, then*). No one *wants* to be a dentist!

KIP. I don't even know why I became one.

BERNADETTE. For the same reason as everyone else! You didn't have the grades for medical school.

KIP. Do you know what teeth are?

BERNADETTE. That's a rhetorical question, I assume.

KIP. They're millstones around my neck.

BERNADETTE. They are?

KIP. Yes.

BERNADETTE. Teeth?

KIP. They're dragging me down, into a vat of dire ugliness.

BERNADETTE. Teeth?

KIP. I look into mouths all day, and if I felt anything I'd burst into tears. I never mentioned it because I try to be positive.

BERNADETTE. Try harder.

KIP. I spend my life staring into gaping, gagging crypts filled with blood and drool.

BERNADETTE. That's very descriptive.

KIP (*excited*). I used to think I could make the mouth my canvas. I thought I could create the universe in miniature. But there is no poetry in teeth. When I was a child I saw things! I went to the museum with my mother. She dragged me from room to room, whispering into my ear the stories of the saints in the paintings. When I could, I ran off and found a room with a bench in the middle. I curled up and fell asleep. Then I opened my eyes. I saw a painting: *The City Rises* by Boccioni. It was beautiful, a

60

scene of chaos with fire and horses and people in panic made up of a million splatters of color. And I stared at it. I studied it. And the colors came alive! Do you understand?

BERNADETTE. You had a dream.

KIP. I didn't! I don't know what it was, but it wasn't a dream! I told my father about it, that night at dinner. He broke all my crayons and lined the garbage with my drawing paper. He thought God was dead and I was proof.

BERNADETTE. I've lost the thread.

KIP. He taught me *not to see*.

BERNADETTE. What's the point of this!?

KIP (*after a moment, simply*). Do you love me, Bernadette?

BERNADETTE. Yes.

KIP. We're partners, aren't we?

BERNADETTE. Yes. Can we please go to bed?

KIP (*grandiose*). I'm going to be a painter! I want to learn to see again. I think it's possible.

BERNADETTE. That's what this is all about?

KIP. Don't belittle my rebirth!

BERNADETTE. Fine. Paint if you want. Paint until your arms fall off.

KIP. I mean full-time.

BERNADETTE. Pardon me?

KIP. I've looked into my last mouth.

BERNADETTE. You can't be serious!

KIP. You said you loved me. We're partners.

BERNADETTE (*in disbelief*). You're not going to work?

KIP. I'm going to work. I'm going to paint!

BERNADETTE. What kind of work is that?

KIP. Work worth doing. We don't need the money. We have your mother's now, and –

BERNADETTE. Oh my God . . . Oh God. You're just –

KIP. Think of possibilities, Bernadette. You have no imagination.

BERNADETTE. I'm going to cry.

KIP. Do you want to go on like this for the rest of our lives?

BERNADETTE. Yes!

KIP. I want something else. You won't get what you don't want. I want a different kind of life.

BERNADETTE. I DON'T! There's nothing wrong with my life the way it is! I'm going to bed! I'd like to pretend this never happened. We never had this conversation.

KIP. Don't be angry. This is wonderful!

BERNADETTE. I think it's pretty goddamn terrible! I woke up this morning next to my husband, now – who are you?!

KIP. I'm me.

BERNADETTE. You are not! I don't want to talk about it.

KIP. I hoped you'd understand.

BERNADETTE. We'll talk about it in the morning.

KIP. I hoped you'd be happy.

BERNADETTE. I'm going to bed.

(KIP *takes her hand*.)

KIP. Look at me.

BERNADETTE (*angry*). What?

KIP. Everything looks new to me.

BERNADETTE. I'm tired.

(*He touches her face*.)

KIP. I've never seen you at all.

(*He takes her hand. She turns to leave. He doesn't release her*.)

BERNADETTE. Let go of me.

KIP. Your eyes.

BERNADETTE. It's late.

KIP. It's morning.

BERNADETTE. Please.

KIP. Your hair.

BERNADETTE. It's dirty.

KIP. It's perfect.

BERNADETTE. Let go.

KIP. You're beautiful.

BERNADETTE. I'm not.

KIP. To me.

BERNADETTE. You have . . .

KIP. You are.

BERNADETTE. Really lost your mind.

(*He kisses her. It quickly becomes passionate and they sink to the floor, making love. Fadeout.*)

COMMENTARY: Nicky Silver has written a screwball comedy dealing with the serious subjects of guilt, redemption and self-punishment. Kip and Bernadette hate their lives and feel imprisoned by their dysfunctional daily existence. They are both self-centred and egotistical, unwilling and unable to accommodate any opinions that contradict their own. The funeral of his hated mother-in-law proves to be a turning point for Kip. He realises he has been in denial for too long and finally finds the motivation to quit being a dentist. His decision is made easier by the knowledge that Bernadette will soon inherit money from her mother's estate. Notice how Kip's calm conviction comes into conflict with Bernadette's scepticism and scorn. He has experienced a life-enhancing breakthrough; she has not, and absolutely resists being caught up in his fanciful artistic enthusiasms. Despite the serious subject matter there is a darkly farcical quality to the writing – especially whenever teeth are mentioned – and this requires expert timing from the actors. There may be a temptation to make these characters too irritating but you must try to find a sympathetic core, otherwise you will instantly lose your audience's interest and attention.

Shopping and F***ing
Mark Ravenhill

Scene 2. Interview room. London.

For some time, Robbie and his companion, Lulu (both early 20s), have been living with Mark, a former wealthy city type, in a bizarre and sinister ménage à trois. Mark has taken the two of them under his wing, promising, 'I love you both and I want to look after you for ever and ever.' Since then, thanks to Mark's pay packet, they have enjoyed 'Good times. The three of us. Parties. Falling into taxis, out of taxis. Bed.' But Mark has now reached a crisis point where he has run out of money and lost his job. He decides to check himself into a drug rehabilitation centre. This leaves Lulu and Robbie to fend entirely for themselves. Lulu, who has trained as an actress, applies for a job as a TV presenter on a home shopping channel. Brian (late 30s) is the producer of the shopping programme. He is married and has a young son of whom he is extremely proud. It transpires that he pays for his son's private education and prized cello lessons with the money he makes by employing people like Lulu to sell Ecstasy at local raves. As this scene opens, Lulu is in the midst of her audition with Brian and she is completely unaware of his alternative agenda.

(BRIAN *and* LULU *sit facing each other.* BRIAN *is showing* LULU *an illustrated plastic plate.*)

BRIAN. And there's this moment. This really terrific moment. Quite possibly the best moment. Because really, you see, his father is dead. Yes? The father was crushed – you feel the sorrow welling up in you – crushed by a wild herd of these big cows. One moment, lord of all he surveys. And then . . . a breeze, a wind, the stamping of a

64

hundred feet and he's gone. Only it wasn't an accident. Somebody had a plan. You see?

LULU. Yes. I see.

BRIAN. Any questions. Any uncertainties. You just ask.

LULU. Of course.

BRIAN. Because I want you to follow.

LULU. Absolutely.

BRIAN. So then we're . . . there's . . .

LULU. Crushed by a herd of wild cows.

BRIAN. Crushed by a herd of wild cows. Yes.

LULU. Only it wasn't an accident.

BRIAN. Good. Excellent. Exactly. It wasn't an accident. It may have looked like an accident but – no. It was arranged by the uncle. Because –

LULU. Because he wanted to be King all along.

BRIAN. Thought you said you hadn't seen it.

LULU. I haven't.
Instinct. I have good instincts. That's one of my qualities. I'm an instinctive person.

BRIAN. Is that right?

(BRIAN *writes down 'instinctive' on a pad.*)

BRIAN. Good. Instinctive. Could be useful.

LULU. Although of course I can also use my rational side. Where appropriate.

BRIAN. So you'd say you appreciate order?

LULU. Order. Oh yes. Absolutely. Everything in its place.

(BRIAN *writes down 'appreciates order'.*)

BRIAN. Good. So now the father is dead. Murdered. It was the uncle. And the son has grown up. And you know – he looks like the dad. Just like him. And this sort of monkey thing comes to him. And this monkey says: 'It's time to speak to your dead dad.' So he goes to the stream and he looks in and he sees –

LULU. /His own reflection.

BRIAN. His own reflection. You've never seen this?

65

LULU. Never.

BRIAN. But then . . . The water ripples, it hazes. Until he sees a ghost. A ghost or a memory looking up at him. His . . .

(*Pause.*)

Excuse me. It takes you right here. Your throat tightens. Until . . . he sees . . . his . . . dad.

My little one. Gets to that bit and I look round and he's got these big tears in his eyes. He feels it like I do.

Because now the dad speaks. And he says: 'The time has come. It is time for you to take your place in the Cycle of Being (words to that effect). You are my son and the one true King.'

And he knows what it is he's got to do. He knows who it is he has to kill.

And that's the moment. That's our favourite bit.

LULU. I can see that. Yes.

BRIAN. Would you say you in any way resembled your father?

LULU. No. Not really. Not much.

BRIAN. Your mother?

LULU. Maybe. Sometimes. Yes.

BRIAN. You do know who your parents are?

LULU. Of course. We still . . . you know. Christmas. We spend Christmas together. On the whole.

(BRIAN *writes down 'celebrates Christmas'*.)

BRIAN. So many today are lost. Isn't that so?

LULU. I think that's right. Yes.

BRIAN. All they want is something.

And some come here. They look to me. You're looking to me aren't you?

Well aren't you?

LULU. Yes. I'm looking to you.

BRIAN (*proffers plate*). Here. Hold it. Just hold it up beside you. See if you look right. Smile. Look interested.

66

Because this is special. You wouldn't want to part with this. Can you give me that look?

(LULU *attempts the look.*)

BRIAN. That's good. Very good. Our viewers, they have to believe that what we hold up to them is special. For the right sum – life is easier, richer, more fulfilling. And you have to believe that too. Do you think you can do that?

(*Again* LULU *attempts the look.*)

BRIAN. Good. That's very good. We don't get many in your league.

LULU. Really?

BRIAN. No. That really is very . . . distinctive.

LULU. Well. Thank you. Thanks.

BRIAN. And now: 'Just a few more left. So dial this number now.'

LULU. Just a few more left. So dial this number now.

BRIAN. Excellent. Natural. Professional. Excellent.

LULU. I have had training.

BRIAN. So you're . . . ?

LULU. I'm a trained actor.

(BRIAN *writes down 'trained actor'.*)

BRIAN. I don't recognise you.

LULU. No? Well, probably not.

BRIAN. Do some for me now.

LULU. You want me to . . . ?

BRIAN. I want to see you doing some acting.

LULU. I didn't realise. I haven't prepared.

BRIAN. Come on. You're an actress. You must be able to do some acting.

An actress – if she can't do acting when she's asked, then what is she really?

She's nothing.

LULU. All right.

(LULU *stands up.*)

LULU. I haven't actually done this one before. In front of anyone.

BRIAN. Never mind. You're doing it now.

LULU. One day people will know what all this was for. All this suffering.

BRIAN. Take your jacket off.

LULU. I'm sorry?

BRIAN. I'm asking you to take your jacket off. Can't act with your jacket on.

LULU. Actually, I find it helps.

BRIAN. In what way?

LULU. The character.

BRIAN. Yes. But it's not helping me. I'm here to assess your talents and you're standing there acting in a jacket.

LULU. I'd like to keep it on.

BRIAN (*stands*). All right. I'll call the girl. Or maybe you remember the way?

LULU. No.

BRIAN. What do you mean – no?

LULU. I mean . . . please, I'd like this job. I want to be considered for this job.

BRIAN. Then we'll continue. Without the jacket. Yes?

(LULU *removes her jacket. Two chilled ready meals fall to the floor.*)

BRIAN. Look at all this.

(*They both go to pick up the meals.* BRIAN *gets there first.*)

BRIAN. Exotic.

LULU. We've got really into them. That's what we eat. For supper.

BRIAN. Did you pay for these?

LULU. Yes.

BRIAN. Stuffed into your jacket. Did you pay for them?

LULU. Yes.

BRIAN. Look me in the eyes. Did. You. Pay?

LULU. No.

68

BRIAN. Stolen goods.

LULU. We have to eat. We have to get by. I don't like this. I'm not a shoplifter. By nature. My instinct is for work. I need a job. Please.

BRIAN. You're an actress by instinct but theft is a necessity. Unless you can persuade me that I need you. All right. Carry on. Act a bit more.

No shirt.

LULU. No . . . ?

BRIAN. Carry on without the . . . (what's the . . . ?) . . . blouse.

(LULU *removes her blouse*.)

LULU. One day people will know what all this was for. All this suffering. There'll be no more mysteries. But until then we must carry on working. We must work. That's all we can do. I'm leaving by myself tomorrow . . .

BRIAN (*stifling a sob*). Oh, God.

LULU. I'm sorry. Shall I stop?

BRIAN. Carry on. As you were.

LULU. Leaving by myself tomorrow. I'll teach in a school and devote my whole life to people who need it. It's autumn now. It will soon be winter and there'll be snow everywhere. But I'll be working.

That's all.

(LULU *puts her shirt and jacket on*.)

BRIAN (*wipes away a tear*). Perfect. Brilliant. Did you make it up?

LULU. No. I learnt it. From a book.

BRIAN. Brilliant. So you think you can sell?

LULU. I know I can sell.

BRIAN. Because you're an actress?

LULU. It helps.

BRIAN. You seem very confident.

LULU. I am.

BRIAN. All right then. A trial. Something by way of a

69

test. I'm going to give you something to sell and we're going to see how well you do. Clear so far?

LULU. Totally.

BRIAN. You understand that I am *entrusting* you?

LULU. I understand.

BRIAN. I am entrusting you to pass this important test.

LULU. I'm not going to let you down.

BRIAN. Good.

(BRIAN *reaches for his briefcase and starts to open it.*)

COMMENTARY: This darkly comic drama presents a desolate world in which sex, drugs and junk food take precedence over relationships and conventional morality. The two characters in this scene are both obsessed and desperate, but in quite different ways. At this point in the play, Lulu seems prepared to do anything to make some money and Brian exploits her eagerness and vulnerability. When Brian asks Lulu to take off her top she is more concerned that her stolen heat-and-serve meals will drop out from under her jacket than she is about revealing her breasts. Do you think Brian ever really intended to offer Lulu a job or is the interview merely a front? Brian's interview technique is somewhat unorthodox and has the intensity of an interrogation. Brian is a consummate manipulator whose smarmy manner is tingled with an aura of menace. There is something comically sinister in his obsession with *The Lion King*. For this scene to work in performance you must find a way to make your audience both laugh and squirm. This scene starts in the middle of the conversation between Lulu and Brian; how do you think they got to this point?

(NB A later scene from this play can be found on page 159 of this volume.)

Simpatico
Sam Shepard

Act 3, scene 1. Living room of Carter's Kentucky mansion, very simple set with the impression of wealth.

Vinnie (40s) is 'dressed in a dark blue long-sleeved shirt, dark slacks with no belt. Everything very rumpled as though he's been sleeping in his clothes for weeks . . . with a "Redwing" shoebox tucked under his arm.' Rosie (late 30s) is 'slightly hung over and rumpled'. She is still wearing her robe. Rosie's husband, Carter, and Vinnie have known each other since they were kids. Fifteen years ago they were business partners involved in a California racetrack scam that involved the swapping of two racehorses and the gross sexual blackmail of Simms, the local commissioner of racing. Vinnie still holds the vital evidence that could incriminate his one-time partner and over the years Carter has paid Vinnie to keep him quiet. At the time of the scam Vinnie and Rosie were married but she then eloped with Carter and married him. Vinnie and Rosie have not seen each other since that time. Rosie now leads a life of wealth and comfort with a nanny to look after her two children. Over the years, as Carter has prospered as a horse breeder, Vinnie has become an increasingly reclusive bum, indulging in fantasy detective games. Vinnie summons Carter to his rundown apartment in Cucamonga in California (NB An excerpt from that scene can be found on page 164 of this volume). He lures him with the pretence that he needs his help to deal with a 'major crisis' involving a girlfriend who had him arrested for assault. However, it transpires that Vinnie has decided that the time has come to revenge himself on Carter and this is all part of his warped plot. In this scene, having abandoned Carter in Cucamonga, Vinnie comes unannounced to Carter's house to visit Rosie. This is their first encounter in fifteen years.

ROSIE. Would you like me to take your coat and uh – your package?

VINNIE. No thanks.

ROSIE. If you're wearing a sidearm under there it doesn't matter. We've seen that before around here. Kelly's seen it. It's old hat.

VINNIE. I'm not.

ROSIE. So, you haven't come to do me in then? Splatter my brains all over the carpet in a fit of jealous rage? (*Pause.*) You're a long way from home, Vinnie.

VINNIE. Yeah. I am.

ROSIE. Carter just went out to see you. Did you know that? That's what he said he was up to anyway. You didn't somehow miss him did you? 'Ships in the night'?

VINNIE. No. I saw him.

ROSIE. Oh, good. Did you work things out? I know it's been a long and bitter negotiation.

VINNIE. He said you two were on the outs.

ROSIE. Who?

VINNIE. You and him.

ROSIE (*laughs*). Is that what he said? Just like that? 'On the outs'! Those were *his* words?

(*Pause*).

VINNIE. Is it okay if I – sit down?

ROSIE. Help yourself! *Mi casa es su casa*, Vinnie. You know that. Just like the old days. Nothing's changed.

(VINNIE *sits on edge of sofa, clutching shoebox under his arm.*)

ROSIE. So, what've you got, a bomb in the box or something? Gonna blow us all to Kingdom Come?

VINNIE. I'm not going to hurt you.

ROSIE. You're not still harboring something, are you Vinnie? That's not healthy. That's the kind of thing that leads to cancer and insanity.

VINNIE. I just wanted to see you.

ROSIE. Well, here I am! Still in the bloom of things. I never would've recognized *you* though, Vinnie. You've let yourself go. I was watching you from the window and I was asking myself, 'Now who is this? Who in the world could this be, arriving by taxi, with a package under his arm?' It's not roses, is it, Vinnie? Roses for Rosie?

VINNIE. No.

ROSIE. I didn't think so. Too short for roses. Too compact. Unless you've cut the stems off. Out of spite or something. Wouldn't that be a shame.

VINNIE. So, how did you know?

ROSIE. What.

VINNIE. How did you recognize me?

ROSIE. Oh. The voice. Something in the voice rang a bell. A kind of apologetic menace. I don't know how else to describe it.

VINNIE. I'm not going to hurt you.

ROSIE. I'd feel a lot more reassured if you didn't keep repeating that.

VINNIE. I just want you to know. I didn't come here for that.

ROSIE. Good. That's good news. Now we don't have to talk about it anymore, do we? (*Pause.*) So you met up with Carter then? How did that go?

VINNIE. All right.

ROSIE. He said you were in some kind of an emergency again. He left here in a big rush.

VINNIE. I am.

ROSIE. Still?

VINNIE. Yes. I'm at the end of my rope. I may not look like it but I am.

ROSIE. Well, actually, you *are* looking a little rough around the edges, Vinnie. I didn't want to say anything –

VINNIE. I got arrested.

ROSIE. Oh. That's too bad. When was that?

VINNIE. A while back. Couple weeks ago.

ROSIE. Well, I'm sorry to hear that, Vinnie. What was it this time?

VINNIE. Assault with a deadly weapon. Attempted manslaughter.

ROSIE. You've escalated.

VINNIE. It won't stick. Just – hysterical reaction, is all it was.

ROSIE. It wasn't Carter, was it?

VINNIE. What.

ROSIE. Did you assault Carter?

VINNIE. No. He's safe.

ROSIE. Where is he?

VINNIE. Out there. My place.

ROSIE. How come he's out there and you're here? What's going on, Vinnie?

VINNIE. He's – He took up with a woman out there.

[(*Pause. ROSIE stares at him. KELLY re-enters with a tray and drinks. Pause, as she sets the drinks down on glass table then turns to go. ROSIE stops her.*)

ROSIE. Kelly?

KELLY (*stops*). Yes, mam?

ROSIE. What time are you picking up the kids today?

KELLY. Three o'clock. The usual time.

ROSIE. Doesn't Simon have band practice?

KELLY. No, not today. That's Thursdays.

ROSIE. Oh. Right. Well, look, Kelly, why don't you take them to have ice cream and then go to Toys 'R' Us or something. All right? Just find something to do with them for a little while.

KELLY (*looks at* VINNIE). Okay.

ROSIE. I need to talk with Mr Webb here.

KELLY. All right.

(KELLY *starts to go, then stops. She eyes* VINNIE *then turns to* ROSIE.)

KELLY (*to* ROSIE). Is everything – Are you sure you'll be all right, Mrs Carter?

ROSIE. I'm fine, Kelly. Just go get the kids now. Do as you're told.

(KELLY *eyes* VINNIE *again, then exits. Pause as* ROSIE *and* VINNIE *sip their drinks*.)]

ROSIE. So – he's run off with a woman. Not that I'm shocked or anything. He's been carrying on behind my back since day one.

VINNIE. When *was* that?

ROSIE. What?

VINNIE. 'Day One'.

ROSIE. We're not going to drag that back up out of the dirt, are we, Vinnie? Things happened. One thing led to another. I don't know. It was a long time ago.

VINNIE. But now it's over, right?

ROSIE. What.

VINNIE. You and him?

ROSIE. Apparently so! What're you trying to tell me? He's shacked up with a woman at *your* place and you've come all the way out here to give me the good news?

VINNIE. He met this girl –

ROSIE. A girl! A girl! It's always a girl. Never a woman.

VINNIE. He met this girl in a bar out there.

ROSIE. What a surprise!

VINNIE. I guess she got infatuated with him.

ROSIE. Oh, *she* got infatuated with *him*!

VINNIE. I guess.

ROSIE. And you, very generously, donated your bed to the cause!

VINNIE. No –

ROSIE. And now you've gone out of your way, as a friend, to make sure I understand all the sordid details!

VINNIE (*sudden burst*). HE STOLE MY BUICK,

ROSIE! HE STOLE MY BUICK AND HE STOLE MY WIFE!

(*Pause.* ROSIE *stares at him.*)

ROSIE. You know, for a long time I kept dreading this confrontation. I had little nightmares about it. But now that it's here, it seems dull actually. Stupid.

VINNIE. You could've left me a note or something.

ROSIE. A note!

VINNIE. Something.

ROSIE. Oh you mean like: 'Gone to the 7–11 to get a six-pack. Be right back'?

VINNIE. Something. Not just – disappeared.

ROSIE. We were *all* checking out of there, Vinnie! *All* of us. That was the plan. Remember?

VINNIE. Yeah. I remember.

ROSIE. No contact. No trace of any connection between us.

VINNIE. That was the plan.

ROSIE. It's a little late for regrets.

VINNIE. I just thought maybe you'd –

ROSIE. What?

(*Pause.*)

VINNIE. Come back.

ROSIE. To what? Life on the backstretch? Fifteen-hundred-dollar claimers? I could've set up house in the back of a horse trailer, maybe?

VINNIE. We had fun. We had some fun.

ROSIE. Fun!

VINNIE. Read the Form 'til two in the morning sometimes. Picking long-shots. Clocking works.

ROSIE. Fun.

VINNIE. Slept in the truck bed. Listened to the tin roof flap on that shedrow.

ROSIE. Fun, fun, fun!

VINNIE. You could've called me or something.

ROSIE. What about *you*? Where have you been all this time?

VINNIE. I had no idea where you went.

ROSIE. Come on. You knew where the checks were coming from. You knew the phone number well enough.

VINNIE. I didn't want to – interrupt your life.

ROSIE. Get outa here.

VINNIE. I thought you and Carter were –

ROSIE. What.

VINNIE. Getting along. I mean –

ROSIE. *You're* the one who disappeared, Vinnie. *You're* the one who vanished.

VINNIE. I'm here, now.

ROSIE. Well, isn't that great! Isn't that dandy! Fifteen years later you sneak through my back door with a dumb box and a hang-dog look on your face.

VINNIE. I wasn't sneaking.

ROSIE. What'd you come here for?
(*Pause.*)

VINNIE. I thought maybe I could set things straight.

COMMENTARY: In *Simpatico* Shepard portrays the dissolution of the American dream into a web of lies, corruption and rootless frenzy. Vinnie is a loner fuelled by vindictive vengeance. He is festering with a deep sense of betrayal and isolation and he wants his retribution now. Why do you think he has waited so long to confront Carter? For Vinnie the past overshadows the present. Vinnie, in his warped plan, aims to play on Carter's guilt and fear. What does he really want to get from black-mailing Carter and confronting Rosie. Imagine how Vinnie's pent-up rage and menace have distorted his grasp of reality. Over the years Vinnie's obsession with Rosie has grown as has his sense of betrayal and resentment towards Rosie and Carter. Rosie now leads a cosseted but washed-up existence; like a character from Sartre, she is locked in a hell of her own making. In this scene the audience does not yet know what is in Vinnie's box and why earlier in the play Carter was so eager to get his hands on it. For the actors in this scene it is important that they know that Rosie was involved in the sexual scam that destroyed Simms: she was the trick who was photographed in explicitly sexual photos which Vinnie has stored away in his shoebox over the years. You must retain an incredible tension between the two characters; both verbal and physical violence are just beneath the surface. For Rosie, Vinnie is the last person in the world she wants to see and her sardonic disdain makes him keep his distance. Vinnie tries to provoke her but she just will not be drawn into his frenzy of retribution.

(NB An earlier scene from this play can be found on page 164 of this volume.)

Some Voices
Joe Penhall

Act 1, scene 6. A pub in Shepherd's Bush, west London.

Laura is in her early twenties, Irish and unemployed. She is pregnant by Dave, her possessive thug of a boyfriend. Ray is also in his twenties. In the week following his release from a mental hospital, where he was treated for schizophrenia, he has been living with his older brother, Pete. The hospital has prescribed heavy medication to stabilise his erratic behaviour and mood swings. However Ray, unbeknownst to Pete, stops taking his pills. Pete is harassed and overworked running his restaurant, and he ends up leaving Ray to his own devices. In an earlier scene, Dave grills Laura about the whereabouts of a ring he gave her, arguing that she must have given it to her 'fancy man'. When she flatly denies this, insisting that she has just lost it, Dave starts to beat her up. At this point Ray (who has never met either Dave or Laura before) innocently walks by and tries to intervene to save Laura. Dave wrongly assumes that Ray is Laura's 'fancy man' and then viciously beats him up. Laura ends up taking Ray back to her bedsit where she quickly cleans up his injuries and then sends him packing. In this scene, a couple of days later, Ray finds Laura again in a local pub.

(LAURA *is sitting at a table drinking and smoking a cigarette. Music blasts out.* RAY *wanders over with drink in hand.*)
RAY. Is . . . anybody sitting there?
LAURA. Only if they're very small.
RAY. Can I sit there?
(LAURA *shrugs.* RAY *sits.*)
RAY. All right?
(*Pause.*)

It's nice here. (*Beat.*) All my friends come here. (*Beat.*) They're not here at the moment.

LAURA. I like it.

RAY. It's a friendly place. I like the music they play. It's not old and it's not new. Very few pubs play this type of music nowadays. Are you Irish?

LAURA. What?

RAY. This is an Irish pub.

LAURA. I'm from Limerick.

RAY. Did you know that there is more drunkenness, suicide and madness amongst the Irish in London than any other race on earth?

LAURA. Is that so?

RAY. Yes, well, that's what they say because mostly you see they're away from their family and they're lonely probably and sometimes there's prejudice against 'em because of who they are and they can't get jobs and things but also mainly it's just loneliness. Have you got any family here or are you just on your own?

LAURA. I'm on my own.

RAY. Me too. I just got my brother. Me dad vanished some years ago but there's still my brother. My mother's dead. Cancer I believe.

(*Pause.*)

No cats, no dogs, no – what are they – little hairy things, in a cage . . . I don't have any sisters. Do you have any sisters?

LAURA. Yeh, I've got a couple of sisters.

RAY. And do you like them?

LAURA. They're all right.

RAY. That's good because you have to be able to like your family. You have to be able to trust them but mainly you have to like them. And sometimes you just don't. Sometimes you don't trust anybody. Then again some-times you form a vague attachment/to –

LAURA. I have no idea, no idea at all, what you are talking about. Can you see that?

(*Pause.*)

RAY. Would you like a drink?

LAURA. Look, I'm sorry if it looked like I wanted you to sit down but in fact I really didn't. What I wanted was to be left alone. And I'm not just saying that, I mean it. I don't want to talk to anybody I don't want to see anybody I don't want to fight with anybody I don't want to drink with anybody smile at anybody play Let's Get To Know Each Other I just don't want to know. I'm in a bad mood.

RAY. Well, why'd you come here?

LAURA. Because . . . I'm in a bad mood. Why did you come here?

RAY (*beat*). I was bored.

LAURA. You were bored so you thought you'd come and talk to me.

(**RAY** *shrugs. Pause.*)

RAY. It's nice here. I live round here. My brother he runs a restaurant it's very busy, sometimes I help out.

LAURA. Really.

RAY. Yes, all the time. (*Beat.*) No, never. What happened to your face?

LAURA. What?

RAY. You/all right?

LAURA. Nothing happened.

RAY. That doesn't look like nothing to me. You got quite a shiner. And your lip's all cut. And your arm, look at your arm.

LAURA. I fell out of bed.

RAY. Ah, I'm always falling out of bed. Falling out of bed and walking into doors. You want to get some carpet in that place that way you won't bruise so easy. So so so did you get to your appointment?

(**LAURA** *looks at him then glances around the pub uneasily.*)

81

LAURA. Yes, thank you.

RAY. You must be up the spout then. Am I right?

LAURA. I beg your pardon?

RAY. Is it his then? That fella of yours?

LAURA. Yes it's his all his handiwork just like your nose. Any other/questions?

RAY. I'm surprised people still want to have babies. I find it fascinating. I mean they say you get a special glow and everything when you have a baby. Like a special . . . (*She gets up.*)

LAURA. I have to go.

RAY. Please stay, sit down don't get all –

(RAY *gets up and puts a hand on her arm, she bats it away.*)

LAURA. Don't touch me!

RAY. Sorry!

LAURA. What is wrong with you?

RAY. I just want to get to know you a bit, what's wrong with that?

LAURA. You don't get to know somebody by just walking up to them in a pub and talking absolute friggin' rubbish to them for half an hour.

RAY. What d'you want me to do?

LAURA. Are you simple or wha'?

RAY. I offered you a drink.

LAURA. That is not how it happens.

RAY. Well, how does it happen?

LAURA. I don't know!

RAY. You don't believe me, do you? I like you. I'm not being funny. I thought you liked me seeing as I saved your life and all. I can't do that every day you know, my brother ain't half got the hump. He don't believe me neither.

(*Pause.* LAURA *sighs and sits.*)

RAY. You got nice eyes.

LAURA. I don't believe this.

RAY. Incredible blue like two swimming pools.

82

LAURA. You don't give up, do you?

RAY. Not really/no.

LAURA. I'm not going to sleep with you, you know.

RAY. What?

LAURA. I said ... (*Lowers her voice.*) I'm not going to sleep with you. If that's what you're getting at.

RAY. I don't want you to sleep with me.

LAURA. It's out of the question.

RAY. I didn't ask you to sleep/with me.

LAURA. Because, because –

RAY. I don't want you to sleep/with me.

LAURA. I'm not sleeping with/anybody.

RAY. I don't want you/to.

LAURA. Just at the moment. Sleeping with people is not the answer to/anything.

RAY. I don't want you to sleep with me.

(*Pause.*)

LAURA. And I'm not doing anything else either.

RAY. I don't want you to.

LAURA. Nothing, you understand? Nothing.

RAY. I don't want to.

(*Pause. They look around sheepishly.*)

LAURA. Well, good. I'm glad we got that sorted/out.

RAY. Who said anything about sleeping with you?

LAURA. I just thought that might have been where things were heading.

RAY. Course not. (*Beat.*) I don't like sleeping anyway, it's boring. I've been asleep for too long.

LAURA. You know that's not what/I meant.

RAY. I can't sleep, at night my brother says, 'Go to sleep,' and I can't. I don't want to. I have nightmares.

(*Pause.*)

LAURA. What d'you have nightmares about?

RAY. Strange things. Things are always the wrong colour

83

or the wrong size. Things speaking to me. Like birds. I mean real birds that fly.

LAURA. What's so scary about that? I'd love to have nightmares about birds.

RAY. I scare easily. Well, I can't speak to them, can I? I'm not Doctor fuckin' Doolittle. (*Beat. She laughs a little.*) What about yours?

LAURA. Who said I get 'em?

RAY. You must do.

LAURA. Yeh, well . . . I wake up before anything really bad happens.

RAY. I know that sort and all. Awful.

LAURA. Yeh . . . awful.

(*Pause.*)

I'm/sorry I –

RAY. No, I'm/sorry.

LAURA. I didn't/mean to –

RAY. I just barged/in –

LAURA. No you –

RAY. I –

LAURA. I –

RAY. I'll get the drinks in.

LAURA. Get the drinks in good idea.

RAY. A pint is it?

LAURA. Vodka. Double.

(RAY *gets up hurriedly and goes to the bar.* LAURA *smokes her cigarette. Pause. She fidgets.* RAY *returns and plonks a vodka orange and a beer down.*)

RAY. You shouldn't smoke and drink you know.

LAURA. There's a lot of things I shouldn't do.

RAY. But you still do 'em. Me too. I personally like to live as if I'm gonna die tomorrow.

LAURA. You might do.

RAY. Yeh, yes that's exactly it. That's exactly it.

(*Pause.*)

84

I'm Ray, by the way.

LAURA. Laura.

(*He puts his hand out, they shake. Beat.*)

RAY. Can I have a feel?

LAURA. What?

RAY. Of your . . . of the . . .

(*He indicates her belly.*)

LAURA. Of this?

(RAY *nods.* RAY *puts his hand on her belly.* LAURA *looks straight ahead.* RAY *puts his ear to her belly and listens.* LAURA *looks around awkwardly.*)

COMMENTARY: This is a bleakly comic play about schizophrenia. Ray has been released from the closeted safety of the asylum into a nightmare world full of rage and madness. He is a figure of troubled charm, displaying an innocent chivalry towards Laura. The actor playing Ray must allow the knowledge of his schizophrenia to inform his performance without telegraphing a 'mad' or 'crazy' demeanour. His illness manifests itself in a gentle boyishness and an engaging verbosity. Ray is a sensitive, pleasant lad tortured by his illness but determined to prove his own resilience. Laura also displays a strong resilient streak; but why do you think she allows Dave repeatedly to abuse her? She is wary of Ray and reacts to him with a mixture of compassion and prickly defensiveness. Laura has a deep sense of fear and pain which makes her wary of Ray's 'friendly' overtures. The actor playing Laura must be careful to balance her obvious irritation with Ray with a genuine tenderness.

Two
Jim Cartwright

One Act. A pub in the north of England.

Moth (40) comes to the pub before his girlfriend Maudie (late 30s). He is a compulsive flirt and drives Maudie to distraction. Maudie yearns desperately for commitment in their relationship but Moth is reluctant to settle down. Moth is permanently broke and relies on Maudie to subsidise his life. She is patient and long-suffering. While waiting for Maudie, he is trying to chat up a girl at the bar. As this scene begins his attempted seduction is interrupted by Maudie's arrival.

(MAUDIE *has entered and taps him on the shoulder*.)

MAUDIE. Hiyah Moth.

MOTH. What are you doing here?

MAUDIE. I'm your bleeding bird aren't I?

MOTH (*looking round*). Yes, yes, but . . .

MAUDIE. Moth. Moth she wasn't interested.

MOTH. How do you know that?

MAUDIE. Believe me I know. Moth, Moth do you still love me?

MOTH. Of course I do, get them in.

MAUDIE. No, I'm not this time.

MOTH. Eh?

MAUDIE. I've had a good talking to by some of the girls at work today. And they've told me once and for all. I've not to let you keep using me.

MOTH. Using. Using. You sing and I'll dance. Ha! No Maudie you know that's not me. But when I'm broke what can I do, I depend on those that say they love me to care for me. And anyway it's always been our way.

MAUDIE. Stop. Stop now. Don't keep turning me over with your tongue.

MOTH. Maudie, my Maudie.

(*He takes her in his arms, kisses her. She swoons.*)

MAUDIE. Oh here get the drinks in.

MOTH (*he opens handbag*). Ah that sweet click. (*Takes out some money.*) Here I go.

(*He sets off around the other side of bar to get served.*)

MAUDIE. Oh no. No. Look he's off with my money again . . . I said this wouldn't happen again and here it is, happened. I've got to get me some strength. Where is it? (*Makes a fist and twists it.*) Ah there. Hold that Maudie. Maudie, Maudie hold that.

(*MOTH on his way back with the drinks. Bumps into someone. Dolly bird.*)

MOTH. Oops sorry love. Bumpsadaisy. You all right . . .

MAUDIE. Moth!

MOTH. See you. Better get these over to me sister. (*Passing others.*) 'Scuse me. (*Others.*) Yep yep. (*Others.*) Beep beep. Here we go Maud.

MAUDIE. What were you . . . (*Shows fist to MOTH.*)

MOTH (*giving drink*). And here's your speciality.

MAUDIE. Aww you always get it just right. Nobody gets it like you. The ice, the umbrella.

MOTH. Of course. Of course.

(*MAUDIE kisses him.*)

MAUDIE. Oh look. I'm going again. All over you.

MOTH. That's all right, just watch the shirt.

(*They drink. He begins looking around. She looks at him looking around. She makes the fist again.*)

MAUDIE. Look at me will you. Look at your eyes, they're everywhere, up every skirt, along every leg, round every bra rim. Why oh why do you keep chasing women!

87

MOTH. Oh we're not going to have to go through all this again are we petal. Is this the girls at work priming you?

MAUDIE. Yes a bit, no a bit. I don't know. I can't remember now, so much has been said. I just want you to stop it.

MOTH. But you know I can't stop myself.

MAUDIE. But you never even get off with them.

MOTH. I know.

MAUDIE. It's like the girls say, I hold all the cards.

MOTH. How do you mean?

MAUDIE. I'm the only woman on earth interested in you.

MOTH. Well yes, but . . .

MAUDIE. Moth let it all go and let's get settled down.

MOTH. I can't it's something I've always done and I guess I always will. (*Again looking at some women.*)

MAUDIE. No, Moth, no . . . Oh how can I get it through to you.

MOTH (*draining his glass empty*). Drink by drink.

MAUDIE. No way. Buzz off Moth.

MOTH. Come on love, get them in. Let's have a few and forget all this. You pay, I'll order.

MAUDIE. No.

MOTH. But Maudie, my Maudie.

MAUDIE. No, I'm stopping the tap. I shall not be used.

MOTH. Used. Used. Well if that's how you feel I can always go you know.

(*He walks down the bar a bit, stops, looks back, walks down the bar a bit, stops, looks back. Falls over a stool. Picks it up, laughs to cover embarrassment, limps back to her.*)

Maudie, I've been thinking, all what you're saying's so true and right as always. I'm losing everything, my flair, my waistline, what's next to go – you? Will it be you next?

MAUDIE (*unmoved*). You'll try anything won't you, just to get into my handbag. The romantic approach, the comic approach, the concern for me approach, the sympathy approach. Does it never end?

MOTH. You forgot sexy in there.

(*She swings for him, he ducks.*)

No Maudie. You're right again. What does a princess like you see in a loser like me?

MAUDIE. I don't know. Well I do. You're romantic, like something on the fade. I love that.

MOTH (*moving in*). Oh Maudie, my Maudie.

(*As he does, she starts to melt again, he starts to reach into her handbag, she suddenly sees this and slams it shut on his hand.*)

MAUDIE. Stop!

MOTH. Aw Maud. How can I prove I'm genuine to you? Here take everything on me, everything, everything. (*Starts frantically emptying his pockets.*) My last 10p, I'm going to give it to you!

MAUDIE. I don't want your poxy ten.

MOTH. You say that now, you say that now Maud, but you don't know what it's going to turn into. I'm going to give you all I've got left. My final, last and only possession. (*Spins and drops it in jukebox.*) My dancing talent.

(*'Kiss' by Tom Jones comes on. MOTH dances.*)

MOTH. 'Cause Maud, whatever you say. Whatever's said and done. I'm still a top dancer 'ant I hey?

MAUDIE. Well you can move.

MOTH. I can Maud. I sure as hell can Maud. (*Dancing.*) I'm dancing for you Maudie. For you only. (*Dancing.*) Come on get up here with me.

(*She comes to him, puts her handbag on the floor, they dance.*)

MOTH. Who's lost it all now eh?

(*He really grooves it.*)

MAUDIE (*worried, embarrassed*). Moth.

MOTH. Come on doll.

MAUDIE. Moth take it easy.

MOTH. Come on. Swing it. Let your backbone slip.

Yeah let your ... Awwwwwww Ow ow!!! (*Stops. Can't move.*)

MAUDIE. Moth, oh God, what is it?

MOTH. Me back, me back. Help oh help.

MAUDIE. What can I do! What can I do!

MOTH. Get me a chair, get me a gin.

MAUDIE (*feeling up his back*). Where is it? Where is it?

MOTH. There between the whiskey and the vodka.

MAUDIE. Ooo another trick, you snide, you emperor of snide! (*Hits him.*)

MOTH. No, no Maud. Really, you've got it all wrong. It's real. Arwwwwww. Get me to a chair!

MAUDIE. It's real is it you swine?

MOTH. Real. Real.

MAUDIE. Real is it?

MOTH (*nodding*). Arrgh. Arrgh.

MAUDIE. Okay let's test it.

MOTH. How?

(*She takes out a fiver and holds it in front of him. He tries to go for it, but he can't.*)

MAUDIE (*amazed*). It is true. (*Starts circling him.*) Trapped. At last after all these years, I finally have that fluttering Moth pinned down. Ha.

MOTH. Oh Maudie what you gonna do?

MAUDIE. Let's see. Let's see here.

MOTH. Don't muck about how. I'm dying here, arrrgh, dying.

MAUDIE. So if, if, I help, what do I get out of it?

MOTH. Anything! Anything!

MAUDIE. Anything, anything eh?

MOTH. Yes, yes, arrrrgh.

MAUDIE. Okay, make an honest woman of me now.

MOTH. No, never, arrrr.

MAUDIE. Okay, see you love.

MOTH. No. Don't go Maud please.

MAUDIE. Sorry love, have to, love to stay but . . . 'bye. And any of you try to help him, you'll have me to deal with, and my handbag.

(MAUDIE *blows him a kiss as she goes. Exits.*)

MOTH. MAUD! Will you marry me?

MAUDIE (*coming back*). Sorry?

MOTH. Will you marry me?

MAUDIE. YES! OH YESSSSSSSSS! (*She comes running to him and hugs him.*)

MOTH (*she's hurt his back*). AARRRRGHHHH!

MAUDIE. Oh sorry love.

(*Still in embrace she guides him to a stool.*)

MOTH. A a aa a.

(*She props him against stool and bar, he is stiff like a board.*)

MOTH. Ah.

MAUDIE. Oh. Oh. (*Cuddling him.*) Oh. (*Suddenly serious.*) Do you still mean it?

MOTH. I mean it. I mean it. Singleness is all over for me.

MAUDIE (*hugging him again as best she can*). Oh Moth you won't regret this.

MOTH. Arrgh. I know. I know.

MAUDIE. I'll get us a taxi. Hold on now. Be brave. You poor thing.

(*She rushes out.*)

MOTH (*turns to girl at front*). You're beautiful you. Look at you. You're fantastic you.

(*Blackout.*)

COMMENTARY: Each scene in this poignantly comic play captures a host of characters as they pass through their local pub. The playwright reveals very little about each of these personalities. Moth is a down-market Don Juan. He flutters around women who attract him like a flame. He thinks of himself as a youthful Casanova, but in this scene he discovers he's creaky and middle-aged. He's got what he thinks is a very good line in romantic banter and chat-up lines. Maudie likes to think she is immune to all this; she's heard it a hundred times before and is not going to be seduced by his 'tongue'. She is down-to-earth, knows what she wants and speaks her mind. This evening she has come to the pub resolved once and for all to issue an ultimatum to Moth. But notice that as soon as Moth comes on to her with his romantic ways she 'swoons' and gives in to him. Maudie keeps trying to rally herself to her cause and cut Moth off each time he goes for her purse strings. To make this scene really effective you must find a subtle balance between the comedy and a genuine feeling for the plight of both Maudie and Moth.

The Woman Who Cooked Her Husband
Debbie Isitt

Scene 5. Hilary and Kenneth's house somewhere near Liverpool, England.

Hilary (40s) 'is dressed in a green taffeta outfit, green tights and shoes. She wears her hair in a beehive.' She is an expert cook and homemaker. Her husband, Kenneth (40s), is an ageing Teddy boy with a passion for Elvis Presley. 'His costume is a green taffeta drape coat with black drainpipe trousers.' After nineteen years of marriage, Kenneth embarks on a secret affair with Laura. He is terrified of approaching middle age and this affair makes him feel that 'I can put it off for a good few years, I'm starting again and I feel just like a teenager'. Laura has been pushing Kenneth to leave Hilary, but he wants to wait until the time is 'right'. At the same time, Hilary is beginning to suspect that Kenneth might be having an affair, but when she confronts him he strenuously denies this. Eventually Laura decides to have a showdown with Hilary. Their emotional confrontation ends with Laura announcing that Kenneth is leaving Hilary in favour of Laura. This scene follows soon after as Kenneth arrives home completely oblivious of the drama that has just ensued.

KENNETH. Hi Hilary – I'm home – what's cooking?
HILARY. Have you had a good day at work?
KENNETH. Yep! What about you?
HILARY. I've had a great day.
KENNETH. How come?
HILARY. No reason. I just had a really great day.
KENNETH. What's for dinner? I'm starving.
HILARY. Nothing . . . I'll do you a salad.
KENNETH (*searching*). Where's my album?

93

HILARY. What album?

KENNETH. My *Aloha Hawaii* album.

HILARY. I don't know.

KENNETH. You don't know? Come on, you've spent the day tidying up, you must have moved it.

HILARY. I haven't touched it Kenneth.

KENNETH. Bloody hell!

HILARY. Did anything interesting happen to you today?

KENNETH. What do you mean, 'interesting'? What sort of question is that? What are you getting at with your 'interesting'?

HILARY. Nothing. I like to hear what you get up to.

KENNETH. What's 'get up to'? Why would I want to 'get up' to anything? It's work, a job – what's the matter with you?

HILARY. Nothing's the matter with me.

KENNETH. Always asking weird questions – why don't you just get off my back.

(*Pause.*)

HILARY. Your album's in the bin.

KENNETH. What?

HILARY. I trod on it. It cracked – I threw it in the bin.

KENNETH. For God's sake, woman, that's my best record!

HILARY. You should have put it away.

KENNETH. What's wrong with you, can't you watch where you're putting your big feet?

HILARY. Yes.

KENNETH. On top of everything else now you're accident-prone.

HILARY. It wasn't an accident.

KENNETH. You did it on purpose.

HILARY. Yes.

KENNETH. What do you mean?

HILARY. I trod on your stupid record on purpose.

KENNETH. You broke my record – on purpose!!?

HILARY. I JUST SAID SO, DIDN'T I?

KENNETH. You've got to be joking – people don't go around breaking my things for no reason.

HILARY. I'm not people, I'm your wife, and I had a good reason.

KENNETH. Why?

HILARY. I don't like it.

KENNETH. What?

HILARY. The record. It gets on my nerves.

KENNETH. You don't go around breaking other people's records just because they get on your nerves.

HILARY. I do.

KENNETH. Right. Give me the money.

HILARY. No.

KENNETH. Give me the money to buy a new one.

HILARY. No – get lost.

KENNETH. YOU are completely mental – I can't believe it.

HILARY. Why are you home so late?

KENNETH. The traffic was bad, why do you think? You break my record, you haven't cooked dinner, you give me the third degree on what I do every minute of the day – God knows why I married you.

(*Pause.*)

HILARY. I saw Laura today.

(*Pause. In the background, the Rossini Overture plays, indicating KENNETH's emotional panic.*)

KENNETH. Who?

HILARY. Laura – you don't know her. Someone I met once at a party.

KENNETH. Oh yeah? What, like an old friend?

HILARY. Not really a friend. More an acquaintance.

KENNETH. Yeah? . . . And?

HILARY. Nothing.

95

KENNETH. Nothing?

HILARY. Nothing.

KENNETH. Fine.

HILARY. How long has it been going on?

KENNETH. What?

HILARY. How long?

KENNETH. I don't know what you're talking about.

HILARY. It could have been going on for years.

KENNETH. WHAT!?

HILARY. You could have been sleeping with me, eating with me, pretending to be faithful to me for years and years – you might at least let me know when it started.

KENNETH. Please, Hilary – I don't know what you mean.

(HILARY *begins pushing him out of her side of the house. He walks backwards, tripping up the steps, refusing to be forced out.*)

HILARY. Have there been any others? Come on, let's hear it, how many have you slipped it into?

KENNETH. Eh . . .

HILARY. Why, Kenneth? Is it my body that repulses you? My personality? The way I speak – what?

KENNETH. You're – you're . . . hysterical! You don't know what you're saying.

HILARY. Hysterical? I'm not hysterical . . . I want you out. Out of this house tonight – I want you to get out and stay out – you can pack a bag and that's all – you take nothing – do you hear – nothing – everything in this house is mine, it's mine – it's all I've got and I'm keeping it – you've got her – now go . . .

(*During the following dialogue – until the blackout – the Rossini Overture increases in volume until it drowns out their voices so we only see the hysteria as she shouts at him to go.*)

KENNETH. Go where?

HILARY. Now Kenneth – quick.

KENNETH. But I don't know what you mean? Have you been drinking?

HILARY. You're a very sad man – very sad.

KENNETH. You can't just throw me out on the street – what am I supposed to have done? You haven't even told me what I've done.

HILARY. Go!

KENNETH. If this is about Laura – I do know a Laura, but nothing's gone on between us – why won't you just talk to me? I hardly know her – there's no way I would have –

HILARY. Just – get – out – of – my – house.

KENNETH. You'll feel different tomorrow – I'll call round.

HILARY. How could you – how could you!?

COMMENTARY: This play portrays a high-energy emotional journey. The playwright suggests in her foreword that each character 'has its own route and the action flares when the paths are crossed. Most of the work should be done out of the scene, building up the emotional truth ready to enter the scene so that the actors can just "be" there during the scene . . . The play should be served up at a fast, furious pace with savage emotional input, clear fast thought changes and an innocence that keeps the play alive and real . . . Dialogue exchanged with wit and passion . . . but never completely hiding the pain that runs very deep amongst all three characters.' Hilary has had some time to mull over her revenge. Her new-found knowledge of the true state of affairs has given her an unaccustomed strength. She starts on an ironic note which catches Kenneth off guard but her controlled anger grows into rampant hysteria as Kenneth refuses to confess. Kenneth is slow to catch on that his secret has been revealed. His web of lies and deceit gradually unravels before him. Hilary has obviously decided that she wants Kenneth out of her life and his petulant and childish responses only strengthen her determination. But notice that despite all the provocation and hysteria, Kenneth never actually confesses to his 'crime'. He is evasive and slippery up to the end. As the playwright indicates, you must be careful to orchestrate the emotional crescendo of this scene, observing the pauses and beats as information is revealed and absorbed.

Scenes for Two Men

Beautiful Thing
Jonathan Harvey

Act 2, scene 1. The landing walkway in front of three flats in a
low-rise block in Thamesmead, south-east London, May 1993.
A hot mid-afternoon.

*Jamie is 'nearly sixteen, a plain-looking lad'. He is fatherless and
lives with Sandra, his mother. She is a gregarious barmaid in a local
pub who has a younger lover. Their small flat is part of a densely
populated and grim council estate. Ste, his next-door neighbour, 'is
also sixteen . . . and attractive in a scally way.' Ste is terrorised and
physically abused by his alcoholic father and older brother who expect
him to do the housework and cook for them. To escape the pain of the
mental and physical persecution at home Ste throws himself into all
kinds of sporting activities at school. He dreams of working at a
nearby sports centre. Jamie, who is less outgoing and confident,
bunks off school and is reluctant to play football, and this leads him
into endless run-ins with his mother. Although Ste is a naturally
popular boy, it is Jamie who realises that there is something more
than friendship developing between them. After a particularly vicious
attack by his father, Ste spends the night with Jamie, sharing his bed.
It is Jamie who persuades Ste to abandon their initial top-to-toe
sleeping arrangement for something more intimate. To the strains of
'You are 16 Going on 17' (from* The Sound of Music) *the two boys
enjoy their first gay sexual encounter. The scene here occurs one week
later. 'Jamie is sitting on the step of his flat, with the front door open.
He is cleaning his glasses. Ste comes on from the street. They both
wear school uniform.'*

JAMIE. Hiya.
STE. Oright?
JAMIE. Bunkin' off?

STE. No, I'm at school, what's it look like?

JAMIE. Not like you.

STE. It's only Sports Day.

JAMIE. Not like you to miss a race.

STE. First time for everything.

JAMIE. You're in the relay team.

STE. Yeah, well . . . don't wanna put . . . put strain on me ankle. It's . . . injured in training.

JAMIE. Oh.

STE. S'not the end of the world.

JAMIE. I was gonna stay and watch you, then Miss Penrose said you'd pulled out so I came back here. Told me mum it wan't compulsory. Sports Day.

STE. Thassa big word, innit?

JAMIE. Compulsory? I know.

STE. I been down Tavy Bridge.

JAMIE. Get anything?

STE. Nah, skint.

JAMIE. I aint seen ya. Where you been hiding?

STE. Nowhere.

JAMIE. Knocked for you a few times.

STE. I aint been hiding.

JAMIE. Thought you mighta come round.

STE. I aint been hiding, all right? It's hot, bloody heat wave, Jamie, and you expect me to be indoors?

JAMIE. No, it's just, you know, just a bit weird.

STE. I was out. All right? What's weird about that? I wan' hiding. I was just, you know, out.

JAMIE. Been worried about ya.

STE. Don't be.

JAMIE. Well, I was.

STE. Well, don't be!

JAMIE. Have they. . . ?

STE. No.

JAMIE. What?

STE. Nothing's happened. Yeah? I'm all right. I'm pucker. Everything . . . everything's pucker.

JAMIE. You ain't running coz you're black and blue. That's why, innit? I know. I've seen. That's why you aint in the relay team.

STE. Give it a rest, Jamie.

JAMIE. Oh, things getting better then, are they? Life a bowl o'cherries in the end flat? Daddy laid off the fist work? Or haven't you burnt the tea lately?

STE. I said, leave it out.

JAMIE. You're scared.

STE. I aint scared o'nothin'!

JAMIE. Yeah?

STE. Yeah! Last week, right. I went Woolwich. Comin' out of a shop and there's this geezer in the gutter, pissed out of his skull, lying there. And everyone was just walking past him. I had to step over him. (*Pause*.) And it was my old man. (*Pause*.) Got me thinking on the bus. Why be scared of a bloke who's dead to the world?

JAMIE. When he knocks ten different types o'shite outa ya.

STE. He's an embarrassment. Nothing more, nothing less. Why be scared o'that?

JAMIE. Scared o'being called queer?

STE (*pause*). Are you?

JAMIE (*pause*). Dunno. Maybe. Maybe not.

STE. And are you?

JAMIE. Queer?

STE. Gay.

JAMIE. I'm very happy. (*Pause*.) I'm happy when I'm with you. (*Pause*.) There, I've said it now, haven't I? Go on, piss yourself.

STE. No.

JAMIE. Why not? Don't you think it's funny?

STE. I don't wanna.

JAMIE. I think it's hilarious.

STE. Yeah?

JAMIE. Too right.

STE. Well, why aren't you laughin' then?

JAMIE (*pause*). D'you wanna come round tonight? (*Pause*.) 'No, Jamie, I don't!'

STE. I got a tongue in me head!

JAMIE. Well, say somin' then.

STE. Can't.

JAMIE. Well, say no then.

STE. Let's do somin'.

JAMIE. What?

STE. Let's go to the park and have a kick-about.

JAMIE. Football?

STE. Yeah, go and get your new ball.

JAMIE. What?

STE. Come on, Jamie, I can't hang around here all day, it does me head in.

(JAMIE *disappears inside. He returns quickly with the football* TONY *bought him earlier. He stands in the doorway holding it.*)

STE. Come on then, on the head, son!

(STE *angles to do a header,* JAMIE *keeps the ball.*)

JAMIE. I can't.

STE. Jay . . .

JAMIE. I'm crap.

STE. That's coz you never try.

JAMIE. I hate football.

STE. Just kick it. (JAMIE *tuts and kicks the ball to* STE.) No, you're doing it wrong. Like this. (*Kicks it back to* JAMIE, *demonstrating a proper kick.* JAMIE *kicks it back again.*) Yeah, that's more like it. Keep your foot like this, it's all in the angle.

(*They kick the ball between them.*)

JAMIE. Are you gonna come round then?

STE. I don't know.

JAMIE. Go on. Come round.

STE. Jamie.

(*They carry on kicking as they speak.*)

JAMIE. Is this how Gary Lineker started, d'you think?

STE. What? Like you?

JAMIE. Yeah?

STE. If I remember rightly, Jamie, whenever we had football in juniors, you ran up and down the field playing *Cagney and Lacey.*

JAMIE. Shut up.

STE. You used to row with Neil Robinson over who was gonna play the blonde.

JAMIE. You mean Cagney, Chris Cagney. (*Adopts an American accent, in imitation of Chris Cagney.*) My name's Christine Cagney and . . . and I'm an alcoholic.

STE. You never went near the ball.

JAMIE. Gary Lineker was just the same!

STE. Yeah?

JAMIE. Yeah.

STE. Which one was he then?

JAMIE. Lacey, the fat one.

STE (*laughs*). He aint fat.

JAMIE. I know.

STE. He's pucker.

JAMIE. I know, he's all right, inn'e? (*Giggles, keeps the ball and reverts to his Cagney impersonation.*) I dunno, Mary Beth . . . I . . . I just don't seem to be able to find the right kinda guy. They take one look at me, a cop in a pink fluffy jumper, and just . . . back off.

STE. Oh, Christine Cagney, you make me heart bleed!

COMMENTARY: Jamie and Ste haven't seen each other for a week since their first tryst and there is a palpable tension and awkwardness between them. Jamie is on the offensive; he wants to know just why Ste has been avoiding him, but notice that he doesn't confront him immediately. Only gradually is Jamie forced to reveal his genuine concern for his friend. Something has happened to make Ste wary of seeing Jamie. What is he afraid of? Ste responds to Jamie's intensifying questions with defensive and evasive answers. Why? What is he hiding? Jamie is far more confident and eager to pursue the relationship. Ste seems grumpy, withdrawn and uncommunicative and Jamie keeps goading him on, provoking Ste to confront both Jamie and his own gayness. Here Jamie is in control, note his judicious use of pauses, and his series of questions all designed to elicit a response, any response, from Ste. Jamie has obviously been rehearsing this scene in his mind, thinking what he will say when he next sees Ste. Ste seems reluctant to pursue the relationship. Why? Notice the change in tone when Jamie asks Ste 'Scared o'being called queer?' This is a raw nerve of a different sort as both boys are coming to terms with their feelings for one another and their awakening sense of their own sexuality. There is a definite shift in Ste's favour when he proposes playing football as he becomes the one calling the shots and Jamie is put on the spot. This proves to be a turning point as the two boys start to loosen up and enjoy themselves.

The Cripple of Inishmaan
Martin McDonagh

Act 1, scene 3. The remote island of Inishmaan off the west coast of Ireland. A shore at night. 1934.

Babbybobby Bennett (early 30s) is 'handsome and muscular'. He earns his living from his rowing boat. His wife died a year ago from TB. Billy Claven (17/18) has a crippled arm and leg. He is an orphan and lives with his two 'aunties'. He is a born dreamer and a bit of a romantic. His lively imagination helps him to deal with the boredom and pettiness of life on Inishmaan. News arrives on the island that the Hollywood director, Robert Flaherty, is coming to Inishmore, a nearby island, to film Man of Aran. *Several of Billy's friends are planning to go in Babbybobby's boat 'to be in this film they're filming'. Billy is eager to go too and in this scene he has come to persuade Bobby to include him on the trip. Johnnypateenmike, the old town gossip, has just left after quizzing Bobby about exactly why he was getting his curragh ready and prattling on about the death of Bobby's wife. Bobby begins the scene annoyed and irritated when he is disturbed once again with Billy's arrival.*

[(JOHNNY *stares at* BOBBY *a second, fuming, then storms off.*] BOBBY *continues with the boat.*)

BOBBY (*quietly*). Ya stupid fecking eej. (*Pause. Calling off left.*) Who's that shuffling on the stones?

BILLY (*off*). It's Billy Claven, Babbybobby.

BOBBY. I should've guessed that. Who else shuffles?

BILLY (*entering*). No one, I suppose.

BOBBY. Are your aunties not worried you're out this late, Cripple Billy?

BILLY. They'd be worried if they knew but I snuck out on them.

BOBBY. You shouldn't sneak out on aunties, Cripple Billy. Even if they're funny aunties.

BILLY. Do you think they're funny aunties too, Babby-bobby?

BOBBY. I saw your Aunty Kate talking to a stone one time.

BILLY. And she shouts at me for staring at cows.

BOBBY. Well I wouldn't hold staring at cows up as the height of sanity, Billy.

BILLY. Sure, I only stare at cows to get away from me aunties a while. It isn't for the fun of staring at cows. There *is* no fun in staring at cows. They just stand there looking at you like fools.

BOBBY. Do you never throw nothing at them cows? That might liven them up.

BILLY. I wouldn't want to hurt them, sure.

BOBBY. You're too kind-hearted is your trouble, Cripple Billy. Cows don't mind you throwing things at them. I threw a brick at a cow once and he didn't even moo, and I got him bang on the arse.

BILLY. Sure that's no evidence. He may've been a quiet cow.

BOBBY. He may've. And, sure, I'm not telling you to go pegging bricks at cows. I was drunk when this happened. Just if you get bored, I'm saying.

BILLY. I usually bring a book with me anyways. I've no desire to injure livestock.

BOBBY. You could throw the book at the cow.

BILLY. I would rather to read the book, Bobby.

BOBBY. It takes all kinds, as they say.

BILLY. It does. (*Pause.*) Are you getting your curragh ready there, Babbybobby?

BOBBY. Oh everybody's awful observant tonight, it does seem.

BILLY. Ready to bring Helen and Bartley o'er to the filming?

(BOBBY *looks at* BILLY *a moment, checks out right to make sure* JOHNNY *isn't around, then returns.*)

BOBBY. How did you hear tell of Helen and Bartley's travelling?

BILLY. Helen told me.

BOBBY. Helen told you. Jeez, and I told Helen she'd get a punch if she let anyone in on the news.

BILLY. I hear she's paying you in kisses for this boat-trip.

BOBBY. She is, and, sure, I didn't want paying at all. It was Helen insisted on that clause.

BILLY. Wouldn't you want to kiss Helen, so?

BOBBY. Ah, I get a bit scared of Helen, I do. She's awful fierce. (*Pause.*) Why, would you like to kiss Helen, Cripple Billy?

(BILLY *shrugs shyly, sadly.*)

BILLY. Ah I can't see Helen ever wanting to kiss a boy like me, anyways. Can you, Bobby?

BOBBY. No.

BILLY (*pause*). But so you'd've took the McCormicks without payment at all?

BOBBY. I would. I wouldn't mind having a look at this filming business meself. What harm in taking passengers along?

BILLY. Would you take me as a passenger too, so?

BOBBY (*pause*). No.

BILLY. Why, now?

BOBBY. I've no room.

BILLY. You've plenty of room.

BOBBY. A cripple fella's bad luck in a boat, and everybody knows.

BILLY. Since when, now?

BOBBY. Since Poteen-Larry took a cripple fella in his boat and it sank.

BILLY. That's the most ridiculous thing I've ever heard, Babbybobby.

BOBBY. Or if he wasn't a cripple fella he had a bad leg on him anyways.

BILLY. You're just prejudiced against cripples is all you are.

BOBBY. I'm not at all prejudiced against cripples. I did kiss a cripple girl one time. Not only crippled but disfigured too. I was drunk, I didn't mind. You're not spoilt for pretty girls in Antrim.

BILLY. Don't go changing the subject on me.

BOBBY. Big green teeth. What subject?

BILLY. The subject of taking me to the filming with ye.

BOBBY. I thought we closed that subject.

BILLY. We hardly opened that subject.

BOBBY. Sure, what do you want to go to the filming for? They wouldn't want a cripple boy.

BILLY. You don't know what they'd want.

BOBBY. I don't, I suppose. No, you're right there. I did see a film there one time with a fella who not only had he no arms and no legs but he was a coloured fella too.

BILLY. A coloured fella? I've never seen a coloured fella, let alone a crippled coloured fella. I didn't know you could get them.

BOBBY. Oh they'd give you a terrible scare.

BILLY. Coloured fellas? Are they fierce?

BOBBY. They're less fierce with no arms or legs on them, because they can't do much to ya, but even so they're still fierce.

BILLY. I heard a coloured fella a year ago came to Dublin a week.

BOBBY. Ireland mustn't be such a bad place, so, if coloured fellas want to come to Ireland.

BILLY. It mustn't. (*Pause.*) Ar, Babbybobby, you've only brought up coloured fellas to put me off the subject again.

BOBBY. There's no cripple fellas coming in this boat, Billy. Maybe some day, in a year or two, like. If your feet straighten out on ya.

BILLY. A year or two's no good to me, Bobby.

BOBBY. Why so?

(BILLY *takes out a letter and hands it to* BOBBY, *who starts reading it.*)

BOBBY. What's this?

BILLY. It's a letter from Doctor McSharry, and you've got to promise you'll not breathe a word of it to another living soul.

(*Halfway through the letter,* BOBBY*'s expression saddens. He glances at* BILLY, *then continues.*)

BOBBY. When did you get this?

BILLY. Just a day ago I got it. (*Pause.*) Now will you let me come?

BOBBY. Your aunties'll be upset at you going.

BILLY. Well is it their life or is it my life? I'll send word to them from over there. Ah, I may only be gone a day or two anyways. I get bored awful easy. (*Pause.*) Will you let me come?

BOBBY. Nine o'clock tomorrow morning be here.

BILLY. Thank you, Bobby, I'll be here.

(BOBBY *gives him back the letter and* BILLY *folds it away.*)

COMMENTARY: This play presents a bitterly ironic and often brutal picture of a rural backwater where the news of a goose biting a cat's tail is a major event. Bobby can be violent and aggressive, strong enough when roused to do a serious injury (which we will see him do on several occasions later in the play). Bobby's sole intention is to get his curragh ready, with as few interruptions as possible, in time for the big trip. Bobby seems very set against having Billy in the boat – why is this? Billy is just another annoyance to be dealt with so that he can get on with his work in peace. Billy often affects a naive demeanour, but his rumpled body belies his sharp and ready wit. How does his profound disability affect him? Notice how he defends his love of books – to him they are not potential missiles but are for reading instead. His letter from the doctor contains the information that he is suffering from TB and only has three months left to live: later in the play it turns out that Billy himself forged this letter. Billy has obviously anticipated Bobby's negative response so he has come prepared with this final trump card. He knows that this is just the right bit of emotional blackmail to use with Bobby. Billy's intention is to ensure that he has a place on Bobby's boat for the trip to Inishmore and he is willing to go to extraordinary lengths to fulfil his ambition. Notice how, despite Bobby's negative reactions, he keeps managing to bring the conversation back to the subject of the trip. Which of the two characters has the upper hand in the conversation – Bobby certainly thinks he does, but is this true? Billy is dogged in his pursuit of Bobby because he desperately wants something from him, whereas Bobby only wants to get rid of Billy.

Dealer's Choice
Patrick Marber

Act 1. A restaurant kitchen in London. Early on a Sunday evening in 1996.

Sweeney (30s) is a chef and Mugsy (30s) is a waiter. They have worked together at the same restaurant for the past seven years. It is three months since Sweeney's 'missus' walked out on him, taking Louise, their five-year-old daughter with her. Mugsy, according to his boss, Stephen, is a 'half-wit' and a 'bloody idiot'. The two men, Stephen, his son, Carl, and other male staff meet once a week for an all-night game of poker at the restaurant. This scene opens the play. Sweeney 'is in the kitchen preparing food' and Mugsy enters, still wearing his fluorescent cycle clip.

(*Enter* MUGSY.)

MUGSY. Evening, Sween.

SWEENEY. All right, mate.

MUGSY. Hey, Sween, this bloke I know won the lottery.

SWEENEY. Oh yeah?

MUGSY. Yeah, he lives on my street. Eight million quid.

SWEENEY. Reckon he'll bung you a few?

MUGSY. Nahh, he's a stingy bastard. He's bought a Ferrari. Takes his trouty old mum out for a spin. 'Cept it's up on bricks now, kids nicked the wheels.

(*Beat.*)

What I could do with eight million quid . . .

SWEENEY. Lose it?

MUGSY. Oh yeah? Call.

(MUGSY *tosses a coin.*)

SWEENEY. Heads.

(*MUGSY catches the coin and looks at it . . . heads.*)

MUGSY. Bollocks.

(*He hands the coin to* SWEENEY.)

SWEENEY. Business as usual.

MUGSY. Here, Sween, what d'you think?

(*He shows* SWEENEY *his tie.*)

Bought it today, thirty quid.

SWEENEY. It's very nice.

MUGSY. Yeah?

SWEENEY. It's very beautiful.

MUGSY. You taking the piss?

(SWEENEY *examines the label.*)

SWEENEY. Ooh, rayon.

MUGSY. What's rayon?

SWEENEY. Greek – for rip-off.

MUGSY. They said it was silk. Is rayon made of silk?

SWEENEY. All the time.

MUGSY. Good. Is Stephen in?

SWEENEY. Next door.

MUGSY. I've got to have words. D'you want to know why?

SWEENEY. Not really.

MUGSY. Yes you do, you've got a tell, it's in your eyes. You forget you're dealing with a master of the psychological nuance here. I can read you like the proverbial book.

SWEENEY. What 'proverbial' book is that then?

MUGSY. The book of psychological nuance. You OK for tonight?

(*Beat.*)

SWEENEY. No, not playing.

MUGSY. Hallo?

SWEENEY. Goodbye.

MUGSY. What do you mean?

SWEENEY. I mean, I'm not playing tonight.

MUGSY. What do you mean, you're not playing?

SWEENEY. Is this an exam? I mean, I'm – not – playing – poker – tonight.

MUGSY. But you've got to play, if you don't play we're four-handed, Stephen won't play four-handed, there'll be no game.

SWEENEY. I can't play.

MUGSY. We know that.

(SWEENEY *laughs sarcastically*.)

MUGSY. Why can't you play?

(*Beat*.)

SWEENEY. I'm seeing Louise.

MUGSY. You're seeing a dolly bird?

SWEENEY. Louise.

MUGSY. Louise?

SWEENEY. My kid, you prat.

MUGSY. I thought your missus wouldn't let you see her?

SWEENEY. Well, I'm seeing her tomorrow, special dispensation.

MUGSY. Tomorrow's tomorrow, you can play tonight.

SWEENEY. I haven't seen my kid for three months, you could at least pretend to be pleased.

MUGSY (*sarcastic*). Hurrah.

SWEENEY. One dark night some deaf, dumb and blind old hag will spawn *your* child. A stupid, snivelling, scrawny mini Mugsy – then you'll understand responsibility.

MUGSY. And what about your responsibility to poker?

SWEENEY. My Louise is more important. I'm not turning up to see her with red eyes, knackered and stinking of booze.

MUGSY. Don't drink then.

SWEENEY. I'm sorry if it spoils your evening but that's the way it is. Finito. End of story.

MUGSY. Yeah, cheers.

(*Beat*.)

Supposing you win? You could take her somewhere special with the money –

SWEENEY. Mugsy –

MUGSY. Madame Tussaud's, the Chamber of Horrors –

SWEENEY. Mugsy –

MUGSY. Medieval torture through the ages, kids love that.

SWEENEY. SHE'S FIVE.

(*Pause.*)

MUGSY. Call.

SWEENEY. Why d'you bother?

MUGSY. Just call.

(MUGSY *tosses a coin.*)

SWEENEY. Tails.

(MUGSY *looks at it. Tails.*)

MUGSY. Bollocks.

(*He hands* SWEENEY *the coin.*)

You seen Carl?

SWEENEY. No.

MUGSY. He said he'd come in at six, he promised.

SWEENEY. Mr Reliable made you a promise, did he?

MUGSY. He's all right.

SWEENEY. He's a ponce.

MUGSY. He's not a ponce.

SWEENEY. How much does he owe you?

(*Beat.*)

MUGSY. Five hundred.

SWEENEY. Mug.

(*Beat.*)

MUGSY. I've scrubbed the debt anyway.

SWEENEY. You done what?

MUGSY. Fair's fair, can't have debts ... between partners.

SWEENEY. What are you banging on about?

MUGSY. If you must know, I'm banging on about a

restaurant, mate. Me and Carl are going to open a restaurant. French. Maybe Italian. The point is it'll piss all over this place.

SWEENEY. *You're* going to open a restaurant?

MUGSY. Yeah, why not?

SWEENEY. 'Chez Mugsy'?

MUGSY. Oh, very witty.

SWEENEY. A restaurant with Carl?

MUGSY. Stephen dotes on him. He's addicted to him. He'll give us the money to get us started. And then, once we're up and running . . . we dump him.

SWEENEY. Who, Stephen?

MUGSY. No, Carl, we dump Carl.

SWEENEY. Your partner.

MUGSY. It's business.

SWEENEY. Have you told Stephen about this?

MUGSY. No. I'm waiting for Carl to soften him up. Of course, if you were to express an interest, if you were to come and see the premises it might sway Stephen in our favour. I'm talking business, Sween, I'm cutting you in.

SWEENEY. I'm OK here, Mugs.

MUGSY. Seize the day, grasp the nettle.

SWEENEY. Yeah and get stung.

MUGSY. Don't you want to be your own boss?

SWEENEY. And I'd be my own boss if I worked for you?

MUGSY. Exactly.

SWEENEY. You nipple.

(*Pause.*)

So where is this 'restaurant'?

MUGSY. I knew you were interested.

SWEENEY. I'm just making conversation.

MUGSY. Yeah, you're like the Invisible Man, completely transparent.

SWEENEY. He wasn't transparent.

MUGSY. Course he was, he was invisible.

SWEENEY. That's not the same as transparent.

MUGSY. The Invisible Man was invisible, you could see straight through him.

SWEENEY. Clingfilm is transparent.

MUGSY. So?

SWEENEY. The Invisible Man was not made of cling-film.

MUGSY. Course he wasn't, he was made of . . . fuck all. (*Beat.*)

SWEENEY. So where is this 'restaurant'?

MUGSY. Mile End.

SWEENEY. There aren't any restaurants in Mile End.

MUGSY. Exactly.

SWEENEY. No one's got any money in Mile End, it's a shithole –

MUGSY. *Used* to be a shithole, now it's 'up and coming'.

SWEENEY. Says who?

MUGSY. Local estate agents, all of them. I've done my research. They say it's highly desirable, desirable people are moving to Mile End in skip loads.

SWEENEY. Where in Mile End?

MUGSY. Mile End Road.

SWEENEY. It's virtually a motorway.

MUGSY. It's a busy main road granted but that's good, plenty of passing trade.

SWEENEY. Where in the Mile End Road?

(*Beat.*)

MUGSY. It's a secret. First rule of business, Sween; money first, information later. The premises are in a secret location that I will not disclose until the ink upon the deal is dry.

SWEENEY. You've lost the plot.

MUGSY. I *am* the plot. Look, the point is Stephen is more likely to lend us the money if you've had a look.

SWEENEY. Rubbish.

MUGSY. It's true, he respects you.

SWEENEY. He respects you too.

MUGSY. Does he?

SWEENEY. Course he does.

MUGSY. You reckon?

SWEENEY. Course.

MUGSY. I respect him.

SWEENEY. He respects you.

MUGSY. He does, doesn't he. You're right. Yeah . . . maybe I'll have a quick word with him now . . . sow the germ in his mind . . .

SWEENEY. You do that, Mugs, good idea.

MUGSY. You'll see.

SWEENEY. Well, go on then.

MUGSY. I'm going.

(*He has forgotten to remove his fluorescent cycle clip.*)

This is me going, mate, to make my fortune.

SWEENEY. Off you go then.

(*Beat.*)

MUGSY. How long you been working here?

SWEENEY. Same as you, seven years.

MUGSY. Long time . . . seven years . . . itchy. Long time to be in the same place. You see, Sween, the world is divided between winners and losers, between men of vision and men of . . . blindness.

(SWEENEY *exits.*)

MUGSY. Some can stand the heat, others stay in the kitchen.

(*He realises he is alone in the kitchen.*)

I think you know what I'm talking about.

(*He takes out a coin.*)

Call.

SWEENEY (*off*). Heads.

(MUGSY *tosses the coin*).

SWEENEY (*off*). Just leave it on the table.

(MUGSY *looks at the coin.*)
MUGSY. Bollocks.
(*He thinks and then puts the coin in his pocket. He exits into restaurant.*)

COMMENTARY: In this caustically comic play a game of poker is played out in apparently real time on stage. The game becomes a metaphor; revealing the rivalries, obsessions and relationships of the men involved. Mugsy has an engaging, childlike enthusiasm; by contrast Sweeney is cynical and realistic. Mugsy has an almost compulsive need to boast. He loves shopping and acquiring new things, but often gets duped – see the tie episode above. He thinks he's really streetwise and smart. Only a couple of weeks ago in a fit of false bravado he lost three grand to Stephen. He thinks of himself as a bit of a comic and wordsmith but his jokes tend to fall flat. Despite his boasting he is quite insecure and desperately wants Sweeney's interest and approval. Mugsy is a dreamer and an idealist who is utterly convinced that one day he too will win the big one. Sweeney is easily irritated with Mugsy because he knows him too well. Sweeney really does enjoy a game of poker but he's reluctant to join in this particular evening because he's seeing his daughter for the first time in three months and he wants to be 'awake'. He's also afraid that if he loses his winnings from the past week then he won't have any money left to spend on his daughter. Sweeney's preoccupation with his daughter makes him taciturn and short with Mugsy. Notice how reticent and coy Mugsy is about revealing the location of his restaurant site; Sweeney repeats his questions and this helps build the comic tension as his incredulity at Mugsy's scheme grows. Later in the play Mugsy reveals that the premises for his potential restaurant are the Mile End Road public conveniences.

The Life of Stuff
Simon Donald

Scene 12. Respect.
Willie Dobie's 'fairly plush office' in his newly acquired
warehouse building. Glasgow, Scotland.

*Willie Dobie (30s) is a champagne-swigging, small-time gangster. He
runs a corrupt empire of tenement blocks tenanted by 'dolies' who pay
their extortionate rents with DHSS money and 'favours' for Dobie.
He in turn helps them out of the very spots of 'bother' that he has
created in the first place. When the play opens he has had his main
rival, Alec Sneddon, burned alive and is planning a party to
celebrate the acquisition of a new warehouse and his expansion into
the 'substances' market. Imprisoned in the basement of the warehouse
are 'the two pests', Janice and Fraser, she with a missing rent-book
and he with only his underpants, half a shaved head and the promise
of escape to Ibiza for their unwitting complicity in Sneddon's murder.
Davey Arbogast (40-odd) is Dobie's right-hand man, with a
penchant for Frank Sinatra. He is a 'dangerous' man, acting
ruthlessly as Dobie's henchman. Here Dobie describes Arbogast,
'Phenomenal guy, Davey Arbogast. A bona fide self-made man.
Totally. Self-made. Mind you that probably explains why he's such
a mis-shapen fucker. Haha. Dragged himself up from the gutter that
boy did. Got himself educated at the college of Hard Knocks. The
University of Life. Mind you he never graduated because he missed
all his tutorials and the neighbour's dog ate his notes. Eh?' Both men
have spent the afternoon indulging in a dangerous cocktail of drugs
and alcohol, and of the two Dobie is certainly the worse for wear.*

ARBOGAST. I mean you're right and I cannot disagree,
Willie, she's a lovely lookin doll.
DOBIE. She's a princess. And also a sense of humour.

ARBOGAST. Not to be laughed at, Willie.

DOBIE. I know and . . .

ARBOGAST. Can I ask you something?

DOBIE. Fire away, Davey, s'what I'm here for.

ARBOGAST. Have you got things sorted out for this evening?

DOBIE. You know me better than that, son.

ARBOGAST. I know.

DOBIE. Exactly.

ARBOGAST. So what I'm saying is . . . concentrate here because I'm thinking hard about all this myself.

DOBIE. Oh – 'CONCENTRATE!' . . . no on you go . . .

ARBOGAST. Because somebody has to. I want to know if the folk who've got invited . . .

DOBIE. Of course . . .

ARBOGAST. The important folk . . .

DOBIE. Uhuh.

ARBOGAST. That a lot hinges on.

DOBIE (*pouring champagne into his glass*). Our vision, Davey.

ARBOGAST. . . . and those special guests that are going to distribute our product upon whom we depend . . .

DOBIE. A shared dependency. Haha.

ARBOGAST. Uhuh. That when they turn up eventually, they're going to be met with a . . .

DOBIE. One whale of a time.

ARBOGAST. With a semblance of. With something not just . . . With all the ground work done and the problems sorted out.

DOBIE (*proffering a glass*). You joinin me?

ARBOGAST. Willie. Can we talk straight?

DOBIE. Well I can, Davey, but with regard to yourself I have some doubts . . .

(ARBOGAST *steps towards* DOBIE, *fast and angry*.)

ARBOGAST. Well you can cut that shite out for a start –

it's not one of your idiot fuckin dolies you're talking to here.

DOBIE (*squares up to deal with this insubordination*). Now just you steady on a wee minute here . . .

(ARBOGAST *goes Chernobyl meltdown on him, grabbing* DOBIE's *throat in one hand and his scrotum in the other.*)

ARBOGAST. Dont fucking steady on a wee minute here me ya little prick! I have had enough of your arsing around to last me! If you fuck me up in this I will rip out your spinal column. I will swap the brains in your skull with the shite from your bowel. And vice versa! Now is that fathomable for you?

(DOBIE *nods. They pause.* ARBOGAST *dusts him down a little.*)

ARBOGAST. Eh? Good God man.

DOBIE. No you're right. That's perfectly fathomable and I apologise. (*He offers his hand.*) It's not that I dont respect you cause I do. Mutual respect.

ARBOGAST (*pauses*). Willie. Keep things simple eh? (*Takes* DOBIE's *hand but doesn't shake it, just clamps it in a superhuman vice grip.*) Now answer me a question or two. Are you or are you not the man in charge?

DOBIE (*can hardly think for the pain*). Am I or am I not . . . ?

ARBOGAST. . . . the man in charge.

DOBIE. I . . .

ARBOGAST. . . . Yes?

DOBIE. . . . am.

ARBOGAST. You are. Good. Excellent. We know where we stand. Have you, as the man in charge – Seen to your responsibilities?

DOBIE (*can't believe the pain*). Pffew . . . eh . . .

ARBOGAST. What I mean by that, Willie is . . .

DOBIE. Uhuh.

ARBOGAST (*giggles*). It's fuckin funny really, just look at

123

you ya trumped up wee jerk. (*Releasing* DOBIE*'s hand. Leaving* DOBIE *on his knees.*) I'll tell you some news shall I, kiddo.

DOBIE. Uhuh.

ARBOGAST. I mean you've worked dead hard and done well for yourself, nobody's denying you that. There's all your tenements chock full of dolies paying you DHSS money and doing you favours – I mean that's all very commendable. And you've saved up and bought this place. And you've got your own wee tame chemist to make the stuff for you. And you've got Alec Sneddon out the way. Now. Do you know what that all adds up to?

DOBIE. Tell me?

ARBOGAST. A very useful foundation. And so. See I need to know if you're up to your responsibilities. That if you set something in motion you wont let it all just fall apart on your head. On everybody's head. Are we speaking our language?

DOBIE. We are. That is my language you're speaking. I'm just not a hundred per cent sure what you're actually talking about.

ARBOGAST. The thing that has to be done. The two pests in the basement. Now in so far as I took care of things up to here as YOU requested, you now find yourself with the opportunity to tie the whole business up in the one go.

DOBIE. That is the way it seems isnt it.

ARBOGAST. So it is.

DOBIE. Where is it the boy wants his tickets to again?

ARBOGAST (*patiently*). No no no no no no. (*He goes to* DOBIE *and puts his hands on his shoulders.*) No no no no no Willie. Listen to me. You go out to the car park . . .

DOBIE. Should I not be . . .

ARBOGAST. Just! Listen to me a minute.

(*He holds up a bunch of car keys.* DOBIE *takes them.*)

ARBOGAST. Under the front seat of my Volvo you'll find a sawn-off shotgun and you go down to the basement and you shoot the boy first and then you shoot the doll . . .

DOBIE. . . . shoot . . .

ARBOGAST. In the head, then burn the bits.

DOBIE. . . . shoot . . . (*He gulps*.) . . . I could never . . . then burn . . . I couldnt . . .

ARBOGAST. You're a big boy, you'll manage.

DOBIE. Davey . . . Davey I could never . . . You couldnt . . . For God's sake (*He cackles*.) You're some man, Davey I mean everybody knows . . .

ARBOGAST. Everybody knows the doll's been seeing Sneddon and now he's burned to death in the back of his van. And the boy's been doin his nut about his tickets. And the boy was in her room the night Sneddon disappeared. And everybody knows what a mad dog Alec was. So he found out and he would've murdered the boy. But the love birds murdered him first before they ran away together to . . .

DOBIE (*softly*). Ibiza.

ARBOGAST. Ibiza! The very same. (*He goes to the lift*.) And who can blame them for that. A very lovely place this time of the year despite what you read. I've been there myself. Under the front seat, Willie. (*He stands in the lift waiting for* DOBIE's *acquiescence*.) . . . Willie?

DOBIE. Under the front seat. Shoot them in the head. Burn them.

ARBOGAST. I knew it. Same language all along. You just need it spelt out a bit.

(*The door closes. The lift descends*.)

COMMENTARY: Simon Donald presents an idiosyncratic view of Scottish low-life, creating a cast of full-time fantasists, bullshitters and inveterate liars. 'Whatever junk forms in their frontal lobes comes out of their mouths simultaneously. Very little is preconceived. This means that they launch into complex sentences with dependent subclauses lying in wait, ready to give them a syntactical kicking at the earliest opportunity. The language is a wrestling match and the actors must resist the temptation to paraphrase clauses into submission. Characters blurt out truths, gaffes and admissions because they get trapped by their own jangled articulacy. The play is fuelled by drugs, lust, fear and alcohol – none traditionally linked with steadiness of brain . . . The governing engine of the play is fear . . . the higher the stakes and the greater the tension then the funnier the more moving the piece' can become. Arbogast is stone-hearted, leaving a whiff of evil wherever he goes. Who has the upper hand? By the end of the scene the roles are reversed as Arbogast has set Dobie up to do a double murder. Arbogast is eloquently incoherent to Dobie, talking 'our language' in a strangely formal way that only he understands. Dobie's slightly sozzled incomprehension only serves to inflame Arbogast.

The Lisbon Traviata
Terrence McNally

Act 2. Stephen and Mike's 'lean and modern' apartment in
New York City. The room is in much disarray. The present.
Early morning.

*Stephen (mid 30s but looks younger) is 'good-looking. Fair. In trim.
Somewhat closed and guarded in his manner'. He is a highly
respected and talented editor for Knopf, a major New York publisher.
He is infatuated with the world of grand opera; he has a huge
collection of opera records, an encyclopedic knowledge about performances and a passionate devotion to the great operatic divas. Stephen
is gay and has been living with his lover, Mike, for eight years. He
has introduced Mike to opera, but he is a reluctant and unwilling
convert. Mike Deller (early 30s) is 'Handsome, sexual. Dark
clothing. Moves well. Direct manner.' He is a doctor at a New York
hospital and specialises in AIDS-related cases. Six months ago Mike
started a new relationship with Paul, a young graduate student at
Columbia University. Stephen stubbornly refuses to see what is
happening, optimistically believing that Mike and he are still a
couple, and that they are merely going through a 'phase'. Mike has
wanted to spend the night at the apartment with Paul to celebrate
their six-month anniversary. To accommodate them but still maintain face, Stephen arranges to have a date with a 'waiter' and
when this falls through he ends up spending the night on a friend's
sofa. In this scene, the following morning, Stephen returns home
unexpectedly early, surprising Mike and Paul. Stephen is extremely
provocative and bitchy towards Paul. In an act of jealous desperation
he even shows Paul some explicit photos of the two of them from their
early days together. As the tension grows, Stephen blasts the
apartment with a recording of* Wozzeck *and this is the final straw for
Mike who hits Stephen twice, drawing blood. Paul becomes
increasingly irritated and angry, leaving Mike with barely a show of
affection. Stephen's taunting sarcasm grows ever more desperate and*

vicious as he struggles hopelessly to keep Mike for himself. But Mike realises that things have 'really gotten impossible here' and decides then and there to move out of the apartment and sleep on his brother's sofa. As the scene begins 'Mike comes out of the bedroom with a small tote bag and some final articles he will pack in the suitcase.'

MIKE. You have my brother's number?

STEPHEN. Don't go. Please, don't go.

MIKE. Will you be going out to the house this weekend?

STEPHEN. What do you care?

MIKE. I think it will be easier to get my things out if you aren't here.

STEPHEN. So soon? I don't see the hurry.

MIKE. Yes or no?

STEPHEN. If Caballé cancels her recital, yes. If she deigns to put in an appearance, no.

MIKE. When will you know?

STEPHEN. With Caballé it's right down to the wire. Why don't you call her? She's staying at Burger King. (*The phone begins to ring.*) Aren't you going to get that? (*The phone machine is set to answer on the fourth ring.*) That could be him. He could be home by now. I'm not going near it all day. The House of Knopf can think I'm dead. This is like waiting for water to boil. Don't give up on me, Michael. (*The machine picks up, interrupting the fourth ring. MIKE looks at phone, anxious to hear who's calling.*)

PAUL'S VOICE. Mike? It's Paul. Are you there? Do you want to pick up? (MIKE *picks up the phone.*)

MIKE. Paul, where are you? What happened? I think we should, too. How soon? What did you tell them at work? The whole day? Great. I'll be there. (*He hangs up.*)

STEPHEN. Let me guess. He said 'I think we should talk' and you said 'I think we should too.' Now he's calling in sick. You see the effect you have on people? (MIKE *is dialing another number.*)

MIKE. Go to hell.

STEPHEN. Now who are you calling?

MIKE (*into phone.*) This is Dr Deller. Number 52. The blue BMW. Thank you. How soon?

STEPHEN. What did they tell you? Ten minutes? That should be the name of that garage. It's probably the only English they speak. 'Ten minutes.' Please don't go. I don't want him in our car.

MIKE. Fine. I'll take a cab.

STEPHEN. I didn't mean that. You know what I mean. What if we got a bigger apartment? Two bedrooms.

MIKE. Ten bedrooms wouldn't be big enough.

STEPHEN. Does it have to be this morning?

MIKE. It should have been three years ago. You can't love what we've become.

STEPHEN. I don't know how to deal with it!

MIKE. Neither do I.

STEPHEN. I was hoping it would go away or one of us would get used to it or both of us would or a new soprano would come along, another Callas, but I suppose that was too much to ask for, or I could see one of your tricks and not be ripped by jealousy.

MIKE. I thought you were the most terrific looking, acting, everything man I'd ever met.

STEPHEN. Shut up. Please, shut up. Just hold me. Or I could not mind so desperately being stood up by a cute waiter who's too young for me anyway. But at his age and given half a choice in this city of a million of them. I wouldn't want to sleep with me either. You can't leave. No one else will want me.

MIKE. That's not true.

STEPHEN. I look in the mirror and see a young, attractive man but no one else does.

MIKE. You are attractive.

STEPHEN. I said young, attractive. Or I could castrate

myself or I could castrate you or we could just get heavily into salt peter and just pretend that none of this mattered – none of it, none of – get another dog and gracefully grow old together.

MIKE. I don't know what to say, Stephen.

STEPHEN. Sure you do.

MIKE. I can't anymore.

STEPHEN. Sometimes I think this is the most beautiful music ever written. (*He puts the phonograph needle to the beginning of 'Ah, forse lui'.*)

MIKE. I do love you, you know.

STEPHEN. Other times it's the Good Friday Music from *Parsifal*. Or *The Magic Flute*, Pamina's aria, or *Fidelio*, the entire second act.

MIKE. Stephen.

STEPHEN. I heard you. You just don't want to hold my hand when I'm afraid of the dark.

MIKE. I just want to be away from you.

STEPHEN. So you can hold someone else's hand when he's afraid of the dark.

MIKE. You'll be fine without me.

STEPHEN. I won't make it without you.

MIKE. You just think you won't.

STEPHEN. Don't tell me what I think. I'll tell you what I think and what I think is this: you're leaving me at a wonderful moment in our long, happy history of queerness to seek a new mate to snuggle up with right at the height of our very own Bubonic Plague.

MIKE. You'll find someone.

STEPHEN. I don't want someone. No, thank you. I'll stay right here. Those are dark, mean and extremely dangerous streets right now. You can say all you want against Maria, no one's ever accused her of causing AIDS. Renata Scotto, yes; Maria, no.

MIKE. Why can't you be serious?

STEPHEN. It hurts too much, okay? Asshole. Self-centered, smug, shit-kicking, all-his-eggs-in-one-basket, stupid asshole. (*He goes to the stereo and moves the needle to Callas singing the recitative leading to 'Sempre Libera' beginning with 'Follie, follie!'*)

MIKE. That's not going to make it hurt any less.

STEPHEN. Shut up! Shut up and listen to this. The least you can do is sit there and listen to one last 'Sempre Libera' with me. 'Always free!', that's you, Michael.

MIKE. I don't want to.

STEPHEN. It's from the by-now-almost-legendary Lisbon *Traviata*.

MIKE. I don't care if it's the Hoboken one.

STEPHEN. Mendy would kill to hear Maria sing this.

MIKE. I'm not Mendy! I've spent the past half-hour trying to get through to you; I've spent the past eight years. You live in *Tosca*. You live in *Turandot*. You live in some opera no one's ever heard of. It's hard loving someone like that.

STEPHEN. Maria does this phrase better than anyone.

MIKE. Listen to me! Turn that down and listen to me.

STEPHEN. It's hard loving someone like me! (*He turns up the volume to a painfully loud level. Callas is all we can hear. MIKE tries to move past STEPHEN who pushes him back.*) Where are you going?

MIKE. Let me go. (*STEPHEN pushes MIKE again and picks up the pair of scissors MIKE had previously used to destroy the Polaroids. He will brandish them to keep MIKE from moving.*)

STEPHEN. You love him, don't you?

MIKE. I said, let me go.

STEPHEN. You're not getting past me.

MIKE. Come on, Stephen, put those down. I'm not staying here with you. (*He takes a step forward. STEPHEN forces him back with the scissors.*)

STEPHEN. You're going to him. You do love him.

MIKE. Yes. I love him.

STEPHEN. Then you don't love me anymore? Then you don't love me anymore?

MIKE. No. I don't love you anymore.

STEPHEN. But I still love you. I adore you.

MIKE. What's the point of this? I have to go. (*Again he tries to move past* STEPHEN *who again forces him back with a violent lunge with the scissors.*)

STEPHEN. I am to lose my life's salvation so that you can run to someone else and laugh at me? You're not going. You're staying here with me.

MIKE. Give way, Stephen.

STEPHEN. I'm not going to warn you again.

MIKE (*stepping forward, opening his arms wide*). All right, do it! Do it or let me by.

STEPHEN (*raising the scissors above his head*). For the last time, will you stay here? (MIKE *holds his hand with the ring in front of* STEPHEN's *face.*)

MIKE. You gave me this ring. (*He pulls it off.*) I don't want it anymore. (*He throws it down.*) Now will you let me by? (MIKE *walks directly past* STEPHEN *who still stands with the scissors raised. Just as* MIKE *passes him,* STEPHEN *grabs him from behind with a cry and pulls* MIKE *towards him.* STEPHEN *stabs* MIKE.) Jesus! (MIKE *begins to fall.* STEPHEN *drops the scissors and helps him to the floor.* STEPHEN *leans* MIKE *back against him.*) Jesus, Stephen, Jesus!

STEPHEN. This part. Listen. No one does it like Maria.

MIKE. I'm hurt. I'm really hurt.

STEPHEN. Listen to that. Brava la Divina, brava.

MIKE. This is real, Stephen!

STEPHEN. I know.

MIKE. Stephen, please, you've got to call somebody. We can't handle this. You killed me.

STEPHEN. We killed each other. People don't just die from this. They die from what you were doing to me. They die from loss.

COMMENTARY: In this play the passions and obsessions of grand opera are played out in a domestic setting. Stephen's love of opera has become so obsessive that he has lost touch with reality. Opera offers a vision of tragic romantic love that eventually overwhelms Stephen. He has become dependent on Mike's love to define who he is and when that love is abruptly withdrawn his world and sense of identity collapse around him. The final realisation that it is really all over for Stephen comes when Mike physically makes his move to leave and it is at this point that Stephen finally loses it. Stephen is plagued with anxieties about his age and sex appeal. Stephen tries to use language and bad jokes as a verbal barrier to prevent Mike leaving the apartment. By contrast Mike's responses are brief and perfunctory; he just wants out. Mike is a realist who knows what he wants and he is all too aware that his relationship with Stephen has passed its sell-by date. He has to deal with real life and death situations in his work; Stephen experiences life and death in the heightened unreal world of grand opera. The crescendo and emotional impact of the music in the scene are crucial, so try and secure a taped recording that you can use and see the difference it makes to the emotional tempo of the scene. This is a highly charged scene that requires great control to build effectively to the horrifying climax. At the end, which mirrors the climax of Bizet's opera *Carmen*, do you think Stephen shows any remorse?

Mojo
Jez Butterworth

Act 1, scene 1. The stockroom at Ezra's Atlantic Club on Dean Street in Soho, London. 1958. Late evening.

Sidney Potts (20s) and Sweets (20s) both work for Ezra in his nightclub. What they actually do is never specified; they are glorified hangers-on and professional sidekicks. They are guarding the door to Ezra's office as big-time Sam Ross is making his pitch for a share of Silver Johnny, the seventeen-year-old English Elvis, who makes 'polite young ladies come their cocoa in public'. Earlier in the scene, Potts's big moment comes when he takes a tray of tea into Ezra's office. Since then, the two men have been analysing every clue about the set-up in Ezra's office. They are both high on pills and alcohol. Ezra's son, Baby, has just left as this scene starts.

SWEETS. Do you think he knows?
POTTS. What do you think?
SWEETS. Ezra wouldn't tell him.
POTTS. He couldn't find the gents in this place without asking.
SWEETS. Ezra wouldn't tell him. Ezra wouldn't trust him.
POTTS. Ezra wouldn't trust him to run a tub. He doesn't know.
SWEETS. If you don't know you don't know.
POTTS. Good. Good. The end. (*Pause.*) Sweets. I heard 'fifty-fifty'.
(*Pause.*)
SWEETS. Okay. Say that again.
POTTS. I don't know.
SWEETS. Okay. Just that little last bit again.

POTTS. I don't know.

SWEETS. You heard fifty-fifty. You said you heard fifty-fifty.

POTTS. I don't know. Don't turn it into nothing. Don't knit a blanket out of it.

SWEETS. Okay. Stop. Sid. Think. Was it Sam? Did Sam say it?

POTTS. Tricky. With the smoke. I'm pouring tea bent double I heard those words. That word. 'Fifty.' Twice. Fifty. Fifty. Fifty. Five-O. I don't know. And the single word 'America'.

(*They look at each other.*)

SWEETS. Okay. Okay. Okay. All we know –

POTTS. All we know is 'Fish are jumping, and the cotton is high.'

SWEETS. Fish are jumping. Precisely.

POTTS. Good. The end. Talk about something else.

SWEETS. Exactly. Good. Great night.

POTTS. Great night. Exactly. We're fucking made.

SWEETS. My life makes sense.

POTTS. Go upstairs see if there's an angel pissing down the chimney.

SWEETS. My whole fucking life makes sense. (*Pause.*) Hold it. Hold it. We've not been told.

POTTS. Makes no difference.

SWEETS. Have you been told?

POTTS. Have you been told?

SWEETS. No.

POTTS. Exactly. Makes no difference. Because, Sweets –

SWEETS. Exactly.

POTTS. You know? Listen. Because – 'He Got There Alone.'

SWEETS. Exactly. Bullcrap.

POTTS. Meaningless. Never fuckin' happened. Listen. Everybody needs –

SWEETS. I know. I know. Others.

POTTS. Go to the museum.

SWEETS. I will.

POTTS. Go down take a look at any picture Napoleon. Go take a butcher's at the Emperor Half the World. And you'll see it. You'll see. They got a lot of blokes *standing around*. Doers. Finders. Advisors. Acquaintances. Watchers. An *entourage*.

SWEETS. Big fuckers in fur boots. On the payroll.

POTTS. Napoleon's chums. And they're all there. Sticking around. Having a natter. Cleaning rifles. Chatting to cherubs. Waiting. Waiting for the deal to come off.

SWEETS. They weren't there they wouldn't have fuckin' painted them.

POTTS. And how much do *they* know? Do they need figures? Clauses? Amounts? Like every time Napoleon wants to move his army half a mile somewhere more strategic, to the other side of the forest, over there behind those rocks, there's got to be a pow-wow? Bollocks. I'll tell you what he does. He has a *think*. Like he's Paid To Do. He *reflects*. Then he goes 'Right. We're going over here, who's fucking coming?'

SWEETS. Bull's-eye.

POTTS. Just 'cos now he's got a big horse don't mean he don't need chums. He's got big, they've put him on the big pony, his mates go – 'Maybe Napoleon don't want us around no more. Cramping him up. Holding him back . . .' 'Cos one thing Sweets. They've put you in seal-skin boots told you you're Emperor, that's when you need mates. 'Cos one day they're gonna lift you back out, stand you in the snow watch your fucking toes drop off.

SWEETS. Listen. Okay. All we know –

POTTS. All we know is 'Fish are jumping, and the cotton is high.'

POTTS. 'Fish are jumping.' Exactly.

136

POTTS. 'It's a Nice Day' and 'Oh look the Fish are jumping, and will you look how high that cotton's got.' Good. Good. The end. They're going back to his.

SWEETS. Tonight?

POTTS. Billiards. They're going to Sam's house for billiards.

SWEETS. Clover.

POTTS. Knee-deep. Thrashing around in it.

SWEETS. Charging through clover on the golden pony.

POTTS. Please sir show me the way to Meadowland? You're standing on it. Lie down take a nap wake up surrounded by wood nymphs.

SWEETS. Hunker down my woodland beauties.

POTTS. He's got dyed hair.

SWEETS. Who?

POTTS. Sam Ross has got dyed hair.

SWEETS. You're kidding.

POTTS. He's took his hat off wham! Bright yellow dyed hair. Not blond or nothing. Yellow. Like a banana.

SWEETS. I never thought I'd know that. I never thought I'd know that detail.

POTTS. Sweets. Sweets. The shoes. The motherfucking *shoes* on the man.

SWEETS. Buckskin. Hand-stitched.

POTTS. Baby buckskin. Baby fucking hand-stitched bucsin.

SWEETS. Baby fuckin' buckskin handstitched by elves.

POTTS. Baby fucking buckskin.

SWEETS. Baby what? Who *knows* . . . ? (*Laughs.*) Eh? Who fucking *knows*?

POTTS. Something rare. Something rare and soft. Something young, can hardly walk, kill it, turn it inside out –

SWEETS. Unborn pony.

POTTS. That's the one. Still attached. Still in the –

SWEETS. Still in its mother's womb.

POTTS. Asleep in the fucking exactly. Wake it up, rip it out, lah-di-dah, pair of shoes. Bom. It's over. I'm going out.

SWEETS. You don't like it? Who cares? I'm fucking paying.

POTTS. I'm going to speak to him.

SWEETS. Exactly. What?

POTTS. What?

SWEETS. What. You're going to speak to Sam?

POTTS. You don't think I should speak to him?

SWEETS. Yes. No. Yes but let Ezra speak to him first.

POTTS. Like I'm going to burst in there giving it the wide.

SWEETS. I know.

POTTS. Like I'm going to burst in there start swinging my cock around.

SWEETS. Sid –

POTTS. If you think I'm going to do that punch me in the face right now.

SWEETS. I don't have to. I know you.

POTTS. I mean *after*. Let the ink dry.

SWEETS. Exactly. Relax. Sit down.

POTTS. Because I have a position in this.

SWEETS. Exactly. We both do.

POTTS. I mean who fucking discovered the kid?

SWEETS. Right.

POTTS. Fact. One solid gold forgotten fact. Ask Mickey. Up Camden. Luigi's.

SWEETS. Luigi who fucks dogs.

POTTS. Yes. No. Luigi with the daughter. Parkway. With the Italian flag up behind the. The thing behind the . . .

SWEETS. With the daughter. Does the liver and onions.

POTTS. That's him. I'm up doing all the Camden jukes.

Three weeks running Luigi's light on his pennies. Every machine in Parkway is pulling in eight nine quid a week, Luigi's it's one bag, two, three quid if you're lucky. So I say stop having a chuckle, inky pinky blah blah blah you're gonna get a kidney punched out.

SWEETS. Only fucking language they speak.

POTTS. So he's gone, listen, he's gone 'No-one's playing the machine.'

SWEETS. Yeah right.

POTTS. He says. Nobody's playing it.

SWEETS. Like we're in Outer Russia.

POTTS. Like it's the *moon*. Outer Russia. Exactly. He says . . . Listen . . . He says, this is a bit . . . *They're doing it themself*. He says they've got a kid comes in here, gets up in the corner, does it himself. The fucking shake rattle roll himself. I mean. Camden kids?

SWEETS. Micks.

POTTS. Do me a favour.

SWEETS. Micks and Paddies.

POTTS. Do me a good clean turn.

SWEETS. Micks and Paddies and wops who fuck dogs.

POTTS. I'm gonna smack him in the face in front the whole caff.

SWEETS. You should smack him in the face in front the whole caff.

POTTS. He says, listen, he says 'Come back tonight, you'll see.' So I come back tonight. And I take Ezra, Mickey, we're gonna scalp him take the rig back if he's told us a fib. (*Pause.*) Lo and behold.

SWEETS. No.

POTTS. In the corner, all the moves. Doing 'Sixty Minute Man'. Everyone watching. In the corner. A *child*. (*Pause.*) That's what happened. (*Pause.*) I'm not whining.

SWEETS. I know.

POTTS. I'm not bleating. You know, am I supposed to get back in the van doing sums?

SWEETS. You don't think to . . .

POTTS. 'I want xyz. Twenty, thirty, forty per cent.'

SWEETS. You're not some fuckin' vulture.

POTTS. I'm not some fucking *doorboy*. Mickey has a viewpoint. And I have a viewpoint.

SWEETS. Too many viewpoints. Always the way.

POTTS. I'm not bleating. I want what's fucking mine.

SWEETS. I know. And I'm helping you.

POTTS. What am I talking about? Everything?

SWEETS. Not everything. Not everything.

POTTS. Am I talking about *Greed*? No, I'm not. I'm talking about what's due. I'm talking about a fair taste. A nose in the trough. Good. Exactly. The end.

(*Feet on the steps.*)

Don't say nothing. Fish are jumping.

SWEETS. The cotton is high.

COMMENTARY: This play presents a volatile gangland world in cartoon terms. Sweets and Potts are a team. They speak the same argot which, if not carefully played, could easily become impenetrable. They are killing time 'waiting for the deal to come off', dreaming of their share in the action. Imagine how these two chancers, with their brash American aspirations, small brains and filthy minds, would move. What kind of clothes and attitudes would they adopt? You must keep the dialogue moving with the speed of amphetamine, without losing the essence and clarity of what you are saying. They are verbose without being eloquent. They are masters at spinning verbal fantasies and riffs. Potts is concerned to keep in with the main players and not lose out on the rewards he feels are his due for discovering Silver Johnny in the first place. Sweets keeps Potts sweet boosting his morale so that he too can share in the deal. They are both suppressing their excitement and anticipation of the big times they see ahead of them.

The Pitchfork Disney
Philip Ridley

'Night. A dimly lit room in the East End of London: front door with many bolts . . . Everything old and colourless.'

Presley and Haley Stray are twenty-eight-year-old twins. 'Presley is dressed in dirty pyjamas, vest, frayed cardigan and slippers. He is unshaven, hair unevenly hacked very short, teeth discoloured, skin pale, dark rings beneath bloodshot eyes.' They are both chocaholics; their addiction is so extreme that they survive solely on a diet of chocolate. When they were eighteen years old their parents mysteriously 'disappeared', and since then their relationship has become increasingly obsessive; they are both still virgins. The only bequest from their parents was a supply of medicine and tranquilisers that they ration between themselves. Always in a state of terror and dread, they experience the world as a living nightmare. Macabre and bizarre fantasy defines their existence. Although they are in their late twenties they regress and behave like children: it is as if the clock stopped for them when they were ten years old. They live hermetically together in a fortified home, shunning all contact with the outside. Cosmo Disney (18) is 'pale with blond hair, and a menacing, angelic beauty'. He is wearing 'black trousers and black patent leather shoes with a bright red, rhinestone and sequin jacket. It is dazzling in the colourless room. He also wears a white shirt and black bow tie.' Disney works as an 'artiste' in a nightclub where he performs an extremely eccentric act. His sole ambition is to make lots of money. This evening, as part of his act, he has been eating razor blades which has caused him intense pain. Driving home from the nightclub he stops his car so that he can be sick in the street. It happens to be outside Presley and Haley's house. When Presley describes what is happening outside Haley completely freaks out and Presley administers some tranquilisers that send her to sleep. With hysterical Haley sedated, Presley invites Cosmo in. Cosmo promptly vomits on the floor and Presley clears up after him. Presley is attracted by Cosmo's colourful, confident and cynical manner, while everything about Presley repulses Cosmo. In this scene, Cosmo starts challenging Presley about his love life. Once he is convinced that Presley has never had one with either men or women, he allows Presley to quiz him about his work.

PRESLEY. I'd . . . still like to know what you do. For a job.

COSMO. Just objective interest?

PRESLEY. Just objective interest.

(*Pause. COSMO stares at PRESLEY. Then COSMO clicks into action. He looks round him. Goes into the kitchen. PRESLEY watches uneasily.*)

PRESLEY (*warily*). What you doing?

COSMO. Looking for something.

PRESLEY. What?

COSMO (*immersed in his search*). We've all got them.

PRESLEY. What?

COSMO (*searching*). You . . . must . . . have . . . some . . . somewhere . . . ? Come on my beauties.

PRESLEY (*worried now*). Will you tell me what you're doing?

COSMO (*finding what he's after*). Ah! Here! Here's one. What a whopper!

(*COSMO enters with whatever he's caught cupped in his hands. He smiles at PRESLEY. PRESLEY smiles nervously back. COSMO – slowly – lets PRESLEY peek at what he's holding.*)

PRESLEY (*stepping back, shocked*). Take it away!

COSMO. Scared?

PRESLEY. Suppose.

COSMO. Why?

PRESLEY. Don't know.

COSMO. Just tell me what it is. Say its name.

PRESLEY. Cockroach.

COSMO. That's right. Cockroach. Costs nothing. Am I right? Cockroaches are free. Am I right?

PRESLEY. Yes.

COSMO. Come here.

(*Pause. Slowly,* PRESLEY *approaches* COSMO.)

COSMO (*parting his hands slightly*). Look at it. Beautiful little thing. They can live on next to nothing. Two grains of soap powder will keep them alive for months. Did you know that?

PRESLEY. No. What you laughing for?

COSMO. Its legs are tickling me. I've got sensitive skin. (*Staring at cockroach.*) Oh, they're little survivors all right. In the event of a nuclear war, the cockroach alone will survive.

PRESLEY (*shocked*). That can't be true.

COSMO. It's true, Mr Chocolate. No one believes me but that doesn't make it a lie. (*Pause.*) I perform in pubs, in clubs, anywhere people will pay me. Some nights I get through a hundred of these things.

PRESLEY. What do you do?

(*Pause.* COSMO *eats cockroach.* PRESLEY *steps back, horrified.* COSMO *swallows cockroach and grins.*)

COSMO. Scared?

PRESLEY (*softly*). Yes.

COSMO. Why?

PRESLEY. Don't know.

COSMO. No one does. It scares them but they love it. That's why they pay. I eat other things as well – caterpillars, maggots, worms, beetles, moths, goldfish, slugs, spiders. I suck live snails from shells, bite wriggling eels in two, gnaw heads from live mice. (*Triumphant.*) I've even eaten a live canary, Mr Chocolate.

PRESLEY (*softly*). Don't call me Mr Chocolate.

(*Pause.* COSMO *stares at* PRESLEY. PRESLEY *is shuffling uncomfortably.*)

COSMO. Why don't you eat one, Presley?

PRESLEY (*breathlessly*). What?

COSMO. A cockroach. Go on. That would make you part of it all.

PRESLEY. I . . . I don't want to.

COSMO (*caressingly*). Oh, go on, Presley.

PRESLEY (*softly*). No.

COSMO. I'll find it for you. I'll go out there and find one. With my own hands, Presley.

PRESLEY (*softly*). Will you?

COSMO. And it would please me, Presley.

PRESLEY (*softly*). It would.

COSMO. It would. Just let me find one. Shall I do that? Let me find one and we'll take it from there. That's all. No promises. How about it, Presley?

(*Pause.*)

PRESLEY (*softly*). Well . . .

(COSMO *smiles. He goes to the kitchen and searches for another cockroach.* PRESLEY *stares round uneasily.* COSMO *returns with a cockroach in his cupped hands. He takes it to* PRESLEY.)

COSMO. It's a nice one, Presley.

PRESLEY (*softly*). Is it?

COSMO. Yes. Take a look. (*Goes to show him.* PRESLEY *flinches away.*) Just one peek. That's all, Presley.

PRESLEY (*nervously*). Just a peek?

COSMO. Just a peek.

(PRESLEY *looks at cockroach.*)

PRESLEY (*breathlessly*). Oh . . . yes.

COSMO. Isn't it a nice one?

PRESLEY. Yes.

COSMO. Juicy.

PRESLEY. Yes.

COSMO. Take another look.

(PRESLEY *looks at cockroach again. Longer this time.*)

PRESLEY. It's very dark.

COSMO. That's right.

PRESLEY. Like a spit of tar.

COSMO. Yes. (*Pause.*) Go on, Presley.

PRESLEY (*nervously*). What?

COSMO. A nibble.

PRESLEY. I . . . can't . . .

COSMO. For me, Presley.

PRESLEY. I . . .

COSMO. It would please me, Presley.

PRESLEY. It would?

COSMO. Very much.

PRESLEY. Kill it first.

COSMO. No. It has to be alive. That's the whole point. (*Pause.* PRESLEY *stares at* COSMO's *cupped hands.*)

COSMO. I'd feel very close to you, Presley. I'd feel as if we shared something. A communion, Presley. (*Opens his hands slightly.*)

(*Very slowly,* PRESLEY *takes the cockroach between his thumb and forefinger. He stares at it.*)

COSMO (*seductively*). Oh, Presley. You don't know how it makes me feel to see you do this.

(PRESLEY *puts cockroach in his mouth and eats it. He hates every moment. Tries to smile.* COSMO *stares at him. Pause.*)

PRESLEY. I need some chocolate. (*Makes lunge for table and starts to devour a bar.*)

(COSMO *clicks out of his 'caressing' mood, grins and goes over to window.*)

PRESLEY (*trying to make light of it*). Made me feel a bit sick.

COSMO. Makes me sick sometimes. What happened tonight. Suddenly got me. Razor blades in my gut. Couldn't walk. I said to Pitch, 'Pitch,' I said, 'you'll have to find the car yourself. I'm in too much agony.' So off he went. I thought, in a minute I'll puke and I'll feel fine.

That's when this demented lunatic wearing pyjamas shoos me into his house. Bet you wouldn't have cleared that puke up if you knew what it was. (*Laughs.*) Well, I said it wasn't curry, didn't I, Mr Chocolate.

PRESLEY. You think it's funny?

COSMO (*suddenly flat*). Just because I laugh don't mean it's funny. (*Looking through the window.*) Where the fuck is he?

PRESLEY. What does your Mummy think about what you do?

COSMO. Haven't got a Mummy.

PRESLEY. Your Daddy then?

COSMO. No Daddy either.

PRESLEY. No Mummy or Daddy?

COSMO. No.

PRESLEY. Are they dead?

COSMO. No. I was hatched. I never saw my parents. I was hatched from an egg and what you see is all I am. Once I had the skin of a baby and now I got this skin. I unzipped my old skin and threw it away. One day I was shitting my nappy, the next I was earning money. I had no childhood.

PRESLEY. I had a lovely childhood.

COSMO. It's all you've had. The world is full of people like you. Ancient children addicted to their chocolate. Ancient children with no vocation.

PRESLEY (*sarcastically*). And what's *your* vocation?

COSMO (*angrily, picking up money*). This!

COMMENTARY: Cosmo is unsettlingly sensuous without being sexual. His temperamental, vain, egotistical and opinionated manner are all utterly fascinating to Presley. It is as if some exotic bird has shattered the monotony of Presley's dreary world. Despite the ten-year age gap, Cosmo maintains the upper hand in his encounter with both Presley and the audience: notice how often he repeats Presley's name. He enjoys making Presley squirm, and Presley himself is a more than willing dupe. Despite both their protestations to the contrary, there is an unmistakable sexual undertone in their unlikely encounter over a cockroach. It becomes a rite of passage for both of them. In tandem with the dark comedy it is important to maintain an air of danger and excitement in the scene. Cosmo manipulates Presley with suspense, provocation and potential terror. Both actors must keep the audience queasily anticipating just what Cosmo will do next and how will Presley react?

(NB An earlier scene from this play can be found on page 52 of this volume.)

Search and Destroy
Howard Korder

Act One, Scene 9. An office. The present. The United States of America.

Martin Mirkheim (30s) is a small-time Florida businessman. His company, Mirkheim Enterprises, which specialises in 'Circus tours. Booking wrestlers. Polka bands' has serious financial difficulties; Martin now owes $47,000 in corporate taxes. Martin decides to jettison the business and his debts after he becomes a follower of Dr Waxling, a self-help TV guru. Martin acts with the faith of the born-again believer eagerly embracing Waxling's libertarian philosophy of personal empowerment. He decides to channel his energies into producing a movie version of Daniel Strong, *Waxling's novel about limitless possibility. Martin meets Kim Feston (late 30s) at a party in Florida. Martin is attracted to the coolly confident and mysterious Kim and he engages him in conversation about* Daniel Strong. *His host gives no explanation of why he abruptly makes Kim leave his party; however, drugs are mentioned. When Kim leaves he gives Martin his business card, telling him to give him a call when he is next in New York. Martin tracks down Dr Waxling who agrees to let Martin have the rights to* Daniel Strong *but only if he can raise $500,000. When he is finally down to his last few dollars, Martin decides to give Kim a visit in New York. This scene is their first business meeting. Martin is 'wolfing down sandwich. Kim watching him.'*

KIM. Some more?
MARTIN. No, I'm, thank you.
KIM. You're sure.
MARTIN. *Uh*-huh.
KIM. Alright. (*Pause.*) So, Martin.
MARTIN. Yes.

KIM. You're not looking your best.

MARTIN. I've been on the road.

KIM. You called me from where?

MARTIN. The Utah region.

KIM. How is it there?

MARTIN. I don't know, Kim. I . . . Cold. It was cold.

KIM. Well, you're in New York now.

MARTIN. Yes.

KIM. How long you here for?

MARTIN. I don't know.

KIM. Where are you staying?

MARTIN. I don't know.

KIM. How is business?

MARTIN. I don't know. I don't have a business. I don't have anything. (*Pause.*)

KIM. What was it you wanted to see me for, Martin?

MARTIN. Huh?

KIM. When you phoned you said you had to see me.

MARTIN. Yes. (*Pause.*) Do you recall our conversation last month?

KIM. On the terrace?

MARTIN. That's right.

KIM. I do indeed.

MARTIN. I felt we made some sort of connection there. That we believed in the same things. That we knew what was important.

KIM. I'm sure that's absolutely true.

MARTIN. I've experienced some . . . setbacks since we last met. My plan failed. I failed. I won't bore you with the details. I met Dr Waxling. We discussed my proposal at great length and he was very impressed with . . . (*Pause.*) He couldn't see me as a threat. I didn't present myself as a serious threat and so I failed.

KIM. I regret hearing this.

MARTIN. No. No. It was the best thing that could have

happened. Because I'm clean. Now I *know*. It doesn't matter who I am. It doesn't matter what I believe. There's one thing I need. I need to become a threat. I need to become the biggest threat there is. And that's what I'm going to do. (*Pause.*)

KIM. What was it you wanted to see me for?

MARTIN. I need half a million dollars now. Later I'll need much more.

KIM. Uh-huh.

MARTIN. I don't care how I get it.

KIM. Right.

MARTIN. Do you understand what I'm saying?

KIM. No. I guess I don't. (*Pause.*)

MARTIN. Kim. You have a *nice* office.

KIM. Thank you.

MARTIN. You make a lot of money, don't you.

KIM. I'm comfortable.

MARTIN. Do you need any help in, in what you do?

KIM. I usually work best alone.

MARTIN. But if someone presented himself to you who was prepared to take risks, would you find a person like that useful? (*Pause.*)

KIM. You don't know what I do.

MARTIN. I don't care. I mean I do know and it doesn't matter. Whether it's whatever you call it right or wrong, I can't worry about that anymore.

KIM. So this thing that I do, you're saying that you'd like to help me do it, despite its dangers and its possible moral or legal complications?

MARTIN. Yes.

KIM. What is it you think I do? (*Pause.*)

MARTIN. At the party –

KIM. Which party.

MARTIN. On the *terrace*, they asked you to leave 'cause . . .

KIM. Because why?

MARTIN. Because you . . . you're a dealer. Right? A drug dealer. (*Pause.*) Aren't you? (*Pause.*) Kim? (*Pause.*)

KIM. I undertake freelance market analysis for a consortium of Pacific Rim industrial groups.

MARTIN. What?

KIM. Robot systems. Medical equipment. Information retrieval.

MARTIN. No.

KIM. Yes.

MARTIN. No. Oh Jesus. Oh no. God damn it God fucking damn it. What a fuck up I am. What a fuck up loving asshole. What a shiteating fuckhead. Look at me. Look at me. (KIM *looks at him. Pause.*) Kim. I beg your pardon. I've made some very bad assumptions about . . . practically everything. And I . . . Good seeing you. Take care. (*He starts out.*)

KIM. Martin.

MARTIN. Yes.

KIM. I'd like to offer some advice, if I may.

MARTIN. What?

KIM. There is nothing so valuable in life as a sense of perspective. (*Pause.*) I am not what you imagined me to be.

MARTIN. I realize that.

KIM. However, I do know members of my peer group who are. I could arrange for you to meet them. Would you like that?

MARTIN. Yes.

KIM. Alright. (*Pause.*) There are many ways of finding money, Martin. Whatever the climate. Whatever the mood.

MARTIN. This is what has to be done.

KIM. Well, you're a big boy. (*Pause.*) You don't smoke.

MARTIN. No.

KIM. I need the nicotine. (*He takes out a cigarette pack and unwraps it.*) It's a curious time, isn't it. I find it curious. Curious to be alive. And change . . . change is *hard*. Honesty, *very* hard. Leaving your desk . . . that's hard. We're not free, you know. All of this and we're still not free. (*Pause.*) You have faith, don't you.

MARTIN. What?

KIM. Faith. (*Pause.*)

MARTIN. Yes.

KIM. I envy that. (*He lights a cigarette and takes a long drag.*) Yes yes yes. I'm sensing *all* sorts of possibilities.

COMMENTARY: This drolly satiric play presents a sardonic view of the American dream. As this scene starts, the two men have obviously been talking for some time. It could be useful for you to improvise what might have already transpired between the two men. It is only a month since the two men met at the party in Florida, but in that time Martin's fortunes have taken a drastic turn for the worse. Martin's fatuous self-delusion and fervour have now reached a point of desperation. He urgently needs to raise the $500,000 and has no scruples about how he will do this. As far as Martin and the audience are concerned, there is every justification in assuming, as Martin confidently does, that Kim is a drug dealer. Do you think Kim is being honest with Martin, or is he manipulating him? Later in the play Kim certainly has contacts in the drug world and you will need to read the play to make your own decision. They are both trying to maintain the upper hand and their dialogue is used as a form of self-aggrandisement. How far do you think these two characters 'connect'? Notice how Kim's minimal and formal phrases contrast with Martin's up front and desperate pronouncements. It is clear what Martin wants from Kim, but what does Kim want from Martin, what are the 'possibilities'? In the end why does Kim agree to help Martin, or do you think he was planning to all along?

Serving it Up
David Eldridge

Act 2, scene 2. A park in east London. The 1990s.

Sonny (late teens) and Nick (late teens) have been best mates since school. Both 'boys are hard-faced'. Sonny, who is now a skinhead, has always been more dominant and up front than the slightly more reflective Nick. Both live at home with their parents; Sonny's drunken wastrel of a father divides his time between the pub and the track, and his mother works as a cleaner. Nick's father runs the local 'chippie' and physically abuses his wife and son. They've recently been laid off from their jobs at a building site and are now living on their dole money. Nick is beginning to get frustrated with just hanging about and wants 'something to do'. He admits to Sonny that he has even started to read a book; Nick, according to Sonny, has 'got some brains'. Nick has just acquired a red Escort mark two car and is eager to earn some money to do it up. Sonny is in no hurry to get a job since he earns extra cash selling drugs. His latest scam is to sell Anadin dipped in food colour and then pass it off as Ecstasy. Sonny's idea of a great holiday is to go to Spain, get drunk, get laid and 'beat the shit' out of the 'spics'. However, as a kid he dreamed of playing cricket for Middlesex. After an unsuccessful attempt to pull a couple of 'birds' at the pub the boys decide to get drunk. On the way home Sonny sees a 'bloke' with a bag of chips and demands one. When the 'bloke' refuses, Sonny, ignoring Nick's entreaties, starts a vicious fight, which ends with him slashing the guy with a knife. In this scene, a week later, the two lads are hanging out in the local park. Sonny, who would make 'Hitler look like the tooth fairy', has been holding forth with some of his loutish opinions. As this scene starts Nick suddenly decides it's time to be honest with Sonny.

NICK. Sonny.

SONNY. Yeah.

(*Pause.*)

Well, spit it out.

NICK. I . . .

SONNY. What?

NICK. I need a change.

SONNY. What do you mean?

NICK. What do we do?

SONNY. Don't know.

NICK. Sit about.

SONNY. Not all the time.

NICK. Get stoned.

SONNY. It's all right. We have a grin.

NICK. Yeah.

(*Pause.*)

Last Friday. The bloke at the bus stop.

SONNY. That prick with the chips?

(SONNY *laughs.*)

NICK. Yeah.

SONNY. What about him?

NICK. You didn't have to cut him, Sonny.

SONNY. Yes I did. I always cut them.

NICK. No.

SONNY. What the fuck's the matter with you?

NICK. It just pisses me off, that's all.

SONNY. Don't get moody on me, Nick. He was an arsehole. He pulled the blade on me. He deserved it.

NICK. He was all right.

SONNY. No way.

NICK. It weren't about that . . . That, that was about enjoying it, seeing the blood.

SONNY. Don't give me this shit.

NICK. He was screaming like a baby, Sonny, like a baby. All that blood pissing out of his mouth. You enjoyed it.

SONNY. No.

NICK. Yes you did, you loved it, you always do. You always do. That . . . That was . . .

SONNY. Fuck you, Nick!

NICK. That was shit, Sonny, that was shit! And we always do it. We always do it, Sonny! I do it, you do it – it's bad, Sonny, it's bad.

SONNY. Yeah, we do it. We do it, Nick. So fucking what? You should think about where you stand. Who your mates are.

(*Pause.*)

NICK. Yeah. Like I said, I'm pissed off.

(*Long pause.*)

They want someone down the tip to do a bit of refuse collection. I'm thinking of going after it.

SONNY. You don't want that . . .

NICK. Get some work, have a bit of money.

SONNY. You're all right.

NICK. I want to do some normal stuff for a while.

(*Pause.*)

SONNY. It's down to you.

(*A beat.*)

You're a mug if you do though.

NICK. I ain't had me car a week, Sonny. I don't want to sell it, but I can't afford it.

SONNY. You've got things sorted as it is. Bits of pocket money. Live at home, what d'you want to spend your life clearing up shit for?

NICK. I don't know.

(*Pause.*)

SONNY. You. You're my mate, Nick.

NICK. I know, Sonny.

(*Pause.*)

SONNY. Let's go down the pub.

NICK. No, Sonny.

SONNY. Look, if you're a bit hard up, I know a geezer who's got five hundred trips he wants to knock out. I mean that stuff got your car in the first place. You know the new under-eighteen night in Ilford? – Well, I've heard they're crying out for some acid down there.

NICK. Yeah?

SONNY. Yeah. Little kids having their experiments – you'll make a bomb. The only reason I haven't been down there is because they won't let me in.

NICK. You're twenty as it is.

SONNY. It's because of my barnet. Get down there. Gap in the market, Nicky-boy. Use your noddle, mate, make your own luck. Stay on the trips for a couple of months. If it's all going all right start taking a few Es with you. That Escort will be a Porsche by the time you're twenty-one. Gap in the market – serve it up and knock it out, Nicky-boy. Sweet as a nut.

(NICK *looks at his feet*.)

SONNY. You're my mate, Nick.

COMMENTARY: This play depicts a world of bleak frustrations and dead-end options. Much of the lads' loutish behaviour and language seems to be based on the code of the playground, but their lives have changed and Nick is the only one who is aware of this. Sonny still acts like the playground bully, but now he hurts people randomly, just for a laugh. Nick is becoming increasingly appalled by Sonny's violent, yobbish behaviour and in this scene he tries to confront him. Sonny is confident that he has his life nicely 'sorted' and he doesn't want 'moody' Nick to start undermining things with his doubts. Notice how he tries to put him down at every opportunity with a mixture of abuse and sarcasm. Sonny shows a callous disregard for either people or property and is unwilling to accept any guilt or responsibility for his actions. Nick is obviously frustrated with his lot but he believes that he has the power to change his life for the better. It is important to note that Nick is not quite as virtuous as he seems, because, completely unbeknownst to Sonny, Nick has been making out with Sonny's mum.

Shopping and F***ing
Mark Ravenhill

Scene 3. Mark's flat 'once rather stylish, now almost entirely stripped bare'. London.

For some time, Robbie and his companion, Lulu (both early 20s), have been living with Mark, a former wealthy city type, in a bizarre and sinister ménage à trois. Mark has taken the two of them under his wing, promising, 'I love you both and I want to look after you for ever and ever.' Since then, thanks to Mark's pay packet, they have enjoyed 'Good times. The three of us. Parties. Falling into taxis, out of taxis. Bed.' But Mark has now reached a crisis point where he has run out of money and lost his job. He decides to check himself into a drug rehabilitation centre. This leaves Lulu and Robbie to fend entirely for themselves. When Lulu applies for a job as a TV presenter on a home shopping channel (NB This scene can be found on page 64 of this volume) she returns from her interview with a bag of three thousand pounds worth of Ecstasy to sell at local raves. As this scene starts, Robbie has just started counting the tablets when 'Mark enters and watches Robbie, who doesn't see him until –'

MARK. Are you dealing?
ROBBIE. Fuck. You made me –
How long have you – ?
MARK. Just now. Are you dealing?
ROBBIE. That doesn't . . .
(*Pause.*)
So. They let you out.
MARK. Sort of.
(*Pause.*)
ROBBIE. Thought you said months. Did you miss me?

MARK. I missed you both.

ROBBIE. I missed you. So, I s'pose . . . I sort of hoped you'd miss me.

MARK. Yeah. Right.

(ROBBIE *moves to* MARK. *They kiss.*)

(ROBBIE *moves to kiss* MARK *again.*)

MARK. No.

ROBBIE. No?

MARK. Sorry.

ROBBIE. No. That's OK.

MARK. No, sorry. I mean it. Because actually I'd decided I wasn't going to do that. I didn't really want that to happen, you know? Commit myself so quickly to . . . intimacy.

ROBBIE. OK.

MARK. Just something I'm trying to work through.

ROBBIE. . . . Work through?

MARK. Yeah. Sort out. In my head.
We've been talking a lot about dependencies. Things you get dependent on.

ROBBIE. Smack.

MARK. Smack, yes absolutely. But also people. You get dependent on people. Like . . . emotional dependencies. Which are just as addictive, OK?

ROBBIE (*pause*). So – that's it, is it?

MARK. No.

ROBBIE. That's me finished.

MARK. No.

ROBBIE. 'Goodbye.'

MARK. I didn't say that. No. Not goodbye.

ROBBIE. Then . . . kiss me.

MARK. Look . . . (*Turns away.*)

ROBBIE. Fuck off.

MARK. Until I've worked this through.

(*Pause.*)

ROBBIE. Did you use?

MARK. No.

ROBBIE. Right. You used, they chucked you out.

MARK. Nothing. I'm clean.

ROBBIE. So . . . ?

(*Pause.*)

MARK. There are these rules, you see. They make you sign – you agree to this set of rules. One of which I broke. OK?

ROBBIE. Which one?

MARK. It was nothing.

ROBBIE. Come on.

MARK. I told them. It wasn't like that. I put my case / but

ROBBIE. *Tell me.*

(*Pause.*)

MARK. No personal relations.

ROBBIE. Fuck.

MARK. You're not supposed to – form an attachment.

ROBBIE. Ah, I see.

MARK. Which I didn't.

ROBBIE. So that's why / you won't kiss me.

MARK. It wasn't an attachment.

ROBBIE (*pause*). If you were just honest. We said we'd be honest.

MARK. It wasn't like that. I told them 'You can't call this a personal relationship.'

ROBBIE. What was it then?

MARK. More of a . . . transaction. I paid him. I gave him money. And when you're paying, you can't call that a personal relationship, can you? / What would you call it?

ROBBIE. You can't kiss me. You fucked someone / but you can't kiss me.

MARK. That would mean something.

ROBBIE. Who was it?

MARK. Somebody.

ROBBIE. Tell me who.

MARK. He was called Wayne.

ROBBIE. Well . . . get you.

MARK. I just – you know – in the shower. Shower and I . . . Saw his bottom. Saw the hole, you know. And I felt like – I wanted to . . . lick it.

ROBBIE (*pause*). That's it?

MARK. We did a deal. I paid him. We confined ourselves to the lavatory. It didn't mean anything.

ROBBIE. Nothing for afters?

MARK. That's all.

ROBBIE. Just Lick and Go.

MARK. It wasn't a personal relation.

ROBBIE (*lets trousers drop*). Well, if you can't kiss my mouth.

MARK. No. With you – there's . . . baggage.

ROBBIE. Well, excuse me. I'll just have to grow out of it. (ROBBIE *pulls his trousers up. Pause.*)

MARK. I'm sorry.

ROBBIE. Sorry? No. It's not . . . sorry doesn't work. Sorry's not good enough.

(*Pause.*)

MARK. You're dealing?

ROBBIE. Doesn't matter.

MARK. Thought so.

ROBBIE. Listen, this stuff is happiness. Little moment of heaven. And if I'm spreading a little – no a great big fuck-off load of happiness –

(*Pause.* ROBBIE *picks up an E between thumb and fore-finger.*)

MARK. It's not real.

ROBBIE. Listen if you, if this, this . . . planet is real . . . (ROBBIE *takes an E. Pause.*)

Waiting for you. Do you know what it's like – waiting?

Looking forward to this day – for you to . . . And you – Oh, fuck it. Fuck it all.
(ROBBIE *takes another E.*)

COMMENTARY: This darkly comic drama presents a desolate world in which sex, drugs and junk food take precedence over relationships and conventional morality. The two characters in this scene are both obsessed and desperate, but in quite different ways. Although Mark's unexpected return from the clinic momentarily throws Robbie, he immediately expects their relationship to start up again. He desperately wants some proof that Mark still loves him, and his whole sense of himself depends on Mark's validation and affection – symbolised for him by a kiss. Right from the start however, their relationship has been based on selfish needs and not on mutual affection. Notice how petulant and childlike Robbie is compared to the withdrawn and calculating Mark. Robbie wants to know the truth, and although it will inevitably hurt him he will use it as a form of emotional blackmail. By this point Mark has managed to close off his feelings and his relationships have now degenerated into mere transactions. Robbie is angry and confrontational; Mark is numb and withdrawn. How actively do you think Mark wanted to be cured? And why do you think he bothered to come back to see Robbie and Lulu?

Simpatico
Sam Shepard

Act 1. 'A cheap, ground-floor apartment on the outskirts of Cucamonga, California. The apartment is very sparse. A sink piled with dirty dishes . . . A bed with one blanket . . . A pile of dirty clothes at the foot of the bed on the floor . . . The windows look out into black space. No trees. No buildings. No landscape of any kind. Just black.'

Vinnie (40s) is 'dressed in a dark blue long-sleeved shirt, dark slacks with no belt. Everything very rumpled as though he's been sleeping in his clothes for weeks. Bare feet.' He is unemployed. Carter (40s) is 'dressed in a very expensive beige suit, dark tie, brown overcoat slung over one arm . . . his shoes are alligator loafers with little tassels.' The two men have known each other since they were kids in Cucamonga. Fifteen years ago they were con-artists collaborating on a racetrack scam in California. Their elaborate scheme involved not only swapping two racehorses but also sexually blackmailing Simms, the commissioner of racing. Since then Carter has paid Vinnie to keep him quiet. Carter has a new rich life in Kentucky as a successful horse breeder and is a happy family man with kids: Rosie, his wife, was formerly Vinnie's wife, and she and Carter eloped together. Vinnie has become a reclusive bum wrapped up in fantasy detective games. But it is Vinnie who still holds the vital evidence that could incriminate his one-time partner. Vinnie has summoned Carter to his apartment to help him deal with 'some kind of a major crisis'. Vinnie's 'crisis' turns out to be a spot of girl trouble and he wants Carter's help. Cecilia, his girlfriend, has had him arrested on 'multiple charges' including ' "Trespassing." "Invasion of Privacy." And Uh – "Harassment." ' Vinnie wants Carter to persuade Cecilia that he is not crazy; in return for this he will then hand over all the incriminating material to Carter.

CARTER. What do you want from me, Vinnie? I've tried to take care of you. I really have.

VINNIE. Yeah. I guess you have.

CARTER. I mean, I don't know what else to do except give you more money. Buy you stuff. Move you to a different place. What else do you want me to do?

VINNIE. Come clean, Carter. It's real simple.

(*Pause.*)

CARTER. Look – I've got a proposition to make you.

VINNIE. A proposition!

CARTER. I'm prepared to make you an offer. You name me a price. Just name me a price – a *realistic* price and I'll pay you *cash* for all the stuff you've got on me. All the negatives, letters, tapes, whatever you've got. We'll clean this whole mess up, once and for all, and be done with it.

VINNIE. But then we'd never see each other again, Carter.

CARTER. I'm serious, Vinnie! I want to end this thing!

(*Pause.*)

VINNIE. You're the only friend I've got, Carter. I mean – this girl – This girl isn't gonna work out. I can tell she's not gonna work out.

CARTER. You don't know that. All you've got to do is go talk to her. I mean if you've got that much feeling for her –

VINNIE. SHE WON'T TALK TO ME! She had me arrested! It wasn't any fun being arrested! I mean I'm not a criminal!

CARTER. No, you're not.

VINNIE. I'm not a criminal in the common sense!

CARTER. Of course not.

VINNIE. Not like you. I mean, I'm basically innocent. I'm an intrinsically innocent person, Carter!

CARTER. Try to calm down.

VINNIE. All I was doing was trying to impress her. That's all. I might have gone a little overboard with the gun and the handcuffs but I wasn't trying to hurt her. She had no reason to arrest me, Carter!

CARTER. No, she didn't.

(*Pause.*)

VINNIE. It's a terrible thing – trying to replace someone – You know? Trying to find someone to take the place – I mean – see, after Rosie ran off I just kinda – (*Takes a drink.*)

CARTER. She didn't 'run off'.

VINNIE. She didn't?

CARTER. No.

VINNIE. What would you call it?

CARTER. She – eloped.

VINNIE. Oh! 'Eloped'! *That's* what you call it. That's right. 'Eloped'!

CARTER. Well, she didn't 'run off'. That makes her sound sneaky and deceitful. That just wasn't the case.

VINNIE. 'Eloped'. (*Offers* CARTER *a drink.*) Drink?

(CARTER *refuses drink.*)

VINNIE. Takes two to elope, I guess. That must be the difference. If it's only just one person eloping then you might call it 'running off'.

CARTER. You might.

(*Pause.*)

VINNIE. Where – did you elope *to* when you both 'eloped'?

CARTER. You're bound and determined to get it around to Rosie, aren't you. You can't help yourself.

VINNIE. Well, it's the main thing we share in common these days, isn't it, Carter?

CARTER. I didn't come here to talk about Rosie.

VINNIE. I'm just curious. Again. In a state of wonder. I used to wonder about it all the time. It was my constant obsession. I'd wake up with it heavy on my mind. The two of you alone in the Buick. Highway 40 East. Driving through the night with her neck on your shoulder. Tucumcari. Amarillo. The smell of cattle in the feedlots. Oil on the wind. The lights of Memphis twinkling across the placid Mississippi.

CARTER. It wasn't that poetic. Believe me.

VINNIE. No?

CARTER. No! It wasn't. I mean – it may have started off that way –

VINNIE. That was *my* Buick too. You realize that, don't you? *My* Buick and *my* wife.

CARTER. It was *her* choice, Vinnie. I never – (*Stops himself.*)

(*Pause.*)

VINNIE. What? You never what?

CARTER. One thing – just led to another. It was *her* idea to run away together, not mine.

VINNIE. 'Elope'.

(*Pause.*)

CARTER. Yes.

VINNIE. You were a victim of circumstance?

CARTER. Well –

VINNIE. And it all just happened to coincide with our little scam on Simms, I guess. That was convenient.

CARTER. It had nothing to do with that!

VINNIE. My forced exile!

CARTER. She had made it up in her mind a long time before that!

(*Pause.*)

VINNIE. Oh. Is that right?

CARTER. Yes. That's right.

VINNIE. How long before?

CARTER. Look –

VINNIE. How long!

CARTER. I don't know how long! Months maybe.

VINNIE. Months? For months you were both sneaking

167

around! Boffing each other in the back seat of my Buick while I was out steadfastly hustling your dirty work! Preparing the ground for your Big Success!

CARTER. No! It was nothing like that. It came out of nowhere.

VINNIE. One day she just woke up and realized she was with the wrong man? That must've been it, huh? A sudden revelation. That happens sometimes. That happened to me once. A sudden revelation.

COMMENTARY: In *Simpatico* Shepard portrays the dissolution of the American dream into a web of lies, corruption and rootless frenzy. In this scene the audience does not know just why Carter is so concerned to get his hands on the box of evidence that Vinnie has squirrelled away over the years. But later in the play, when, unbeknownst to Carter, Vinnie visits Rosie, it is revealed that Rosie was the 'trick' photographed in the set-up with Simms. This is important information for the actors, explaining why Carter is so eager to get his hands on the negatives since they would irrefutably implicate him and thus destroy his precious new life. Despite having very similar backgrounds these two men couldn't now be more different – or could they? Do you think the differences between them are merely superficial? Vinnie is a loner fuelled by vindictive vengeance. He is festering with a deep sense of betrayal and isolation and he wants his retribution now. Why do you think he has waited so long to confront Carter? For Vinnie the past overshadows the present and for Carter the present is everything. Vinnie, in his warped plan, aims to play on Carter's guilt and fear. What does he really want to get from blackmailing Carter? Imagine how Vinnie's pent-up rage and menace have distorted his grasp of reality. Carter tries, in his slick-suited way, to talk business with Vinnie. But his smooth veneer merely hides how desperate he is for expiation. They are equally obsessive but in different ways. Their dialogue rattles and ricochets all over the place as they each try to get the upper hand.

(NB A later scene from this play can be found on page 71 of this volume.)

Speed-the-Plow
David Mamet

Scene 1. Gould's office in Hollywood. Morning. Boxes and painting materials all around.

Bobby Gould and Charlie Fox are both 'around forty' and they have known one another as friends and business colleagues for eleven years. They have both worked in the film 'biz' all their lives and it completely defines their lives. They love the thrill of it all – the danger, the money and the power play. Gould, who has recently been promoted to Head of Production at a Hollywood film studio, has just moved into his new office. Fox comes to Gould with a proposal for a new buddy prison movie with the hot star, Dougie Brown, who has given him a twenty-four-hour option to close the 'deal'. Gould, realising this is his big chance, instantly phones his boss, Ross, who agrees to meet with them the following morning to discuss the 'deal'. They then strut about hyping each other up with elation and confidence. In this scene they are planning their celebratory lunch.

FOX. Lunch at the Coventry.
GOULD. That's right.
FOX. Thy will be done.
GOULD. You see, all that you got to do is eat my doo doo for eleven years, and eventually the wheel comes round.
FOX. Pay back time.
GOULD. You brought me the Doug Brown script.
FOX. Glad I could do it.
GOULD. You son of a *bitch* . . .
FOX. Hey.
GOULD. Charl, I just hope.

FOX. What?

GOULD. The shoe was on the other foot, I'd act in such a . . .

FOX. . . . hey . . .

GOULD. Really, princely way toward *you*.

FOX. I *know* you would, Bob, because lemme tell you: experiences like this, *films* like this . . . these are the films . . .

GOULD. . . . Yes . . .

FOX. *These* are the films, that whaddayacallit . . . (*Long pause.*) that make it all worthwhile.

GOULD. . . . I think you're going to find a *lot* of things now, make it all worthwhile. I think *conservatively*, you and me, we build ourselves in to split, minimally, ten percent. (*Pause.*)

FOX. Of the net.

GOULD. Char, Charlie: permit me to tell you: two things I've learned, twenty-five years in the entertainment industry.

FOX. What?

GOULD. The two things which are always true.

FOX. One:

GOULD. The first one is: there is no net.

FOX. Yeah . . . ? (*Pause.*)

GOULD. And I forgot the second one. Okay, I'm gonna meet you at the Coventry in half an hour. We'll talk about boys and clothes.

FOX. Whaddaya gonna do the interim?

GOULD. I'm gonna *Work* . . . (*Indicating his figures on the pad.*)

FOX. Work . . . ? You never did a day's work in your life.

GOULD. Oooh, Oooh, . . . the Bitching Lamp is Lit.

FOX. You never did a fucken' day's work in your life.

GOULD. That true?

FOX. Eleven years I've known you, you're either scheming or you're ziggin' and zaggin', hey, I *know* you, Bob.

GOULD. Oh yes, the scorn of the impotent . . .

FOX. I know you, Bob. I know you from the *back*. *I* know what you're staying for.

GOULD. You do?

FOX. Yes.

GOULD. What?

FOX. You're staying to Hide the Afikomen.

GOULD. Yeah?

FOX. You're staying to put those moves on your new secretary.

GOULD. I am?

FOX. Yeah, and it *will* not work.

GOULD. It will not work, what are you saying . . . ?

FOX. No, I was just saying that she . . .

GOULD. . . . she wouldn't go for me.

FOX. That she won't go for you.

GOULD (*pause*). Why?

FOX. Why? (*Pause.*) *I* don't know.

GOULD. What do you see . . . ?

FOX. I think . . . I think . . . you serious?

GOULD. Yes.

FOX. I don't want to pee on your parade.

GOULD. No . . .

FOX. I mean, I'm sorry that I took the edge off it.

GOULD. I wasn't *going* to hit on her.

FOX. Hmmm.

GOULD. I was gonna . . .

FOX. You were gonna work.

GOULD. Yes.

FOX. Oh.

GOULD (*pause*). But tell me what you see.

FOX. What I see, what I *saw*, just an observation . . .

GOULD. . . . yes . . .

FOX. It's not important.

GOULD. Tell me what you see. Really.

FOX. I just thought, I just thought she falls between two stools.

GOULD. And what would those stools be?

FOX. That she is not, just some, you know, a 'floozy' . . .

GOULD. A 'floozy' . . .

FOX. . . . on the other hand, I think I'd have to say, I don't think she is so *ambitious* she would schtup you just to get ahead. (*Pause.*) That's all. (*Pause.*)

GOULD. What if she just 'liked' me? (*Pause.*)

FOX. If she just 'liked' you?

GOULD. Yes.

FOX. Ummm. (*Pause.*)

GOULD. Yes.

FOX. You're saying, if she just . . . *liked* you . . . (*Pause.*)

GOULD. You mean nobody loves me for myself.

FOX. No.

GOULD. No?

FOX. Not in *this* office . . .

GOULD. And she's neither, what, vacant nor ambitious enough to go . . .

FOX. . . . I'm not saying you don't *deserve* it, you *do* deserve it. Hey, . . . I think you're worth it.

GOULD. Thank you. You're saying that she's neither, what, dumb, nor ambitious enough, she would go to bed with me.

FOX. . . . she's too, she's too . . .

GOULD. She's too . . . High-line . . . ?

FOX. No, she's, she's too . . .

GOULD. She's too . . .

FOX. . . . yes.

GOULD. Then what's she doing in this office?

FOX. She's a *Temporary* Worker.

GOULD. You're full of it, Chuck.

FOX. Maybe. And I didn't mean to take the *shine* off our . . .

GOULD. Hey, hey, he sends the cross, he sends the strength to bear it. Go to, go to lunch, I'll meet you at . . .

FOX. I didn't mean to imply . . .

GOULD. Imply. Naaa. Nobody Loves Me. Nobody loves me for myself. Hey, Big Deal, don't go mopin' on me here. We'll go and celebrate. A Douglas Brown Film. Fox and Gould . . .

FOX. . . . you're very kind . . .

GOULD. . . . you brought the guy in. Fox and Gould Present:

FOX. I'll see you at lunch . . . (*Starts to exit.*)

GOULD. But I bet she would go, I bet she *would* go out with me.

FOX. I bet she would, too.

GOULD. No, No. I'm saying, I think that she 'likes' me.

FOX. Yeah. I'm sure she does.

GOULD. No, joking apart, Babe. My *perceptions* . . . Say I'm nuts, I don't *think* so – she likes me, and she'd go out with me.

FOX. How much?

GOULD. How much? Seriously . . . ? (*Pause.*)

FOX. Yeah.

GOULD. . . . that she would . . . ?

FOX. Yeah. That she would *anything*. (*Pause.*) That she would anything. (*Pause.*) That she would deal with you in any other than a professional way. (*Pause.*)

GOULD. Well, my, my, my, my, my.

FOX. What can I tell you, '*Bob*'.

GOULD. That I can get her on a date, that I can get her to my house, that I can screw her.

FOX. I don't think so.

GOULD. How much? (*Pause.*)

FOX. A hundred bucks.

GOULD. That's enough?

FOX. Five hundred bucks that you can't.

GOULD. Five hundred? That's enough?

FOX. A gentleman's bet.

GOULD. Done. Now get out of here, and let me work . . . the Coventry at One. I need . . .

FOX. The script, the budget, chain of ownership . . .

GOULD. Good.

FOX. I'll swing by my, I'll bring it to lunch.

GOULD. Good. Char . . . (*Pause.*)

FOX. What?

GOULD. Thank you.

FOX. Hey. Fuck you. (*Exits.*)

COMMENTARY: This play depicts a dog-eat-dog world where speed, rather than critical judgement, is the essence of every transaction. Even people become commodities and product. Fox and Gould are both merely bit players in the huge Hollywood machine but with their new mindless project they too dream of joining the big-time money boys. Notice how both men use a lot of words to say very little and how their conversation is peppered with Hollywood slang and argot. Their misuse of language gives them a sense of false power and importance. They understand each other even when they talk in staccato shorthand: notice how often they complete one another's sentences. Underneath their apparent camaraderie there are signs of tension and jealousy that gives this scene its particular dynamic.

Play Sources

Beautiful Thing by Jonathan Harvey (Methuen)

The Beauty Queen of Leenane by Martin McDonagh (Methuen)

Boys' Life by Howard Korder in *Boys' Life & Search and Destroy* (Methuen)

Broken Glass by Arthur Miller (Methuen)

Closer by Patrick Marber (Methuen)

The Cripple of Inishmaan by Martin McDonagh (Methuen)

Dealer's Choice by Patrick Marber (Methuen)

Dog Opera by Constance Congdon in *The Actor's Book of Gay and Lesbian Plays* (Penguin)

The Heidi Chronicles by Wendy Wasserstein in *The Heidi Chronicles and Other Plays* (Vintage)

The Life of Stuff by Simon Donald in *Made in Scotland* (Methuen)

The Lisbon Traviata by Terrence McNally (Dramatists Play Service)

The Lodger by Simon Burke (Methuen)

Mojo by Jez Butterworth (Nick Hern Books)

The Pitchfork Disney by Philip Ridley in *Philip Ridley Plays: 1* (Methuen)

Raised in Captivity by Nicky Silver (TCG)

Search and Destroy by Howard Korder in *Boys' Life & Search and Destroy* (Methuen)

Serving it Up by David Eldridge in *Serving it Up & A Week with Tony* (Methuen)

Shopping and F***ing by Mark Ravenhill (Methuen)

Simpatico by Sam Shepard in *Sam Shepard Plays: 3* (Methuen)

Some Voices by Joe Penhall (Methuen)

Speed-the-Plow by David Mamet in *David Mamet Plays: 3* (Methuen)

Two by Jim Cartwright in *Jim Cartwright Plays: 1* (Methuen)

The Woman Who Cooked Her Husband by Debbie Isitt (Warner/Chappell)

Acknowledgements

The editors and publishers gratefully acknowledge permission to reproduce copyright material in this book:
Simon Burke: *The Lodger*. Copyright © 1994 by Simon Burke. Reprinted by permission of Methuen Publishing. Enquiries regarding all performance rights should be addressed to Curtis Brown, 162–168 Regent Street, London WIR 5TB. Jez Butterworth: *Mojo*. Copyright © 1995, 1996 by Jez Butterworth. Reprinted by permission of the publishers Nick Hern Books, 14 Larden Road, London, W3 7ST to whom all enquiries regarding amateur performances should be addressed. Enquiries regarding professional performance rights should be addressed to Curtis Brown, Haymarket House 28–29 Haymarket, London SWI 45P. Jim Cartwright: *Two*. *Two* was first published as *To* in 1991 by Methuen Drama and is reprinted here with corrections. Copyright © 1991, 1994, 1996 by Jim Cartwright. Reprinted by permission of Methuen Publishing. Enquiries regarding all performance rights should be addressed to Judy Daish Associates Ltd, 2 St Charles Place, London WIO 6EG. Constance Congdon: *Dog Opera*. Copyright © 1995 by Constance Congdon. Reprinted by permission of the William Morris Agency, Inc., 1325 Avenue of the Americas, New York, NY 10019. Enquiries regarding amateur performance rights should be addressed to Samuel French Inc., 45 West 25th Street, New York, NY 10010. Enquiries regarding professional performance rights should be addressed to the William Morris Agency, Inc. Simon Donald: *The Life of Stuff*. Copyright © 1992 by Simon Donald. Reprinted by permission of Methuen Publishing. Enquiries regarding all performance rights should be addressed to Hamilton Asper Management Ltd, 76 Oxford Street, London WIN OAT. David Eldridge: *Serving it Up*. First published by the Bush Theatre in 1996. Copyright © 1996,

The editors and publishers have taken all possible care to secure permissions for the extracts used in this volume, and to make the correct acknowledgements. If any errors have occurred, they will be corrected in subsequent editions, provided notification is sent to the publisher.